THE HAMLY
FIFTY-FOUI

D0589263

This book is due for return on or before the last date shown below.

AUSTRALIA
Law Book Co.
Sydney

CANADA and USA
Carswell
Toronto

HONG KONG
Sweet & Maxwell Asia

NEW ZEALAND
Brookers
Wellington

SINGAPORE and MALAYSIA
Sweet & Maxwell Asia
Singapore and Kuala Lumpur

# LEGAL CONUNDRUMS IN OUR BRAVE NEW WORLD

by

## HELENA KENNEDY Q.C.

*Published under the auspices of*
THE HAMLYN TRUST

LONDON
SWEET & MAXWELL
2004

*Published in 2004 by Sweet & Maxwell Limited of
100 Avenue Road, Swiss Cottage,
London NW3 3PF
Typeset by LBJ Typesetting Ltd of Kingsclere
Printed by Athenaeum Press, Tyne & Wear*

No natural forests were destroyed to make this product;
only farmed timber was used and replanted

**A CIP catalogue record for this book is available from the British
Library**

ISBN 0421 851902 (HB)
0421 85250X (PB)

# TABLE OF CONTENTS

| | |
|---|---|
| *The Hamlyn Lectures* | vii |
| *The Hamlyn Trust* | xi |
| *Table of Cases* | xiii |
| 1. Taking Liberties—Terrorism and the Rule of Law | 1 |
| 2. Pandora's Box—Genetics and the Law | 21 |
| 3. The Benign State—A Modern Myth | 39 |
| *Index* | 55 |

# THE HAMLYN LECTURES

1949 Freedom under the Law
    by the Rt Hon. Lord Denning

1950 The Inheritance of the Common Law
    by Richard O'Sullivan, Esq.

1951 The Rational Strength of English Law
    by Professor F.H. Lawson

1952 English Law and the Moral Law
    by Professor A.L. Goodhart

1953 The Queen's Peace
    by Sir Carleton Kemp Allen

1954 Executive Discretion and Judicial Control
    by Professor C.J. Hamson

1955 The Proof of Guilt
    by Professor Glanville Williams

1956 Trial by Jury
    by the Rt Hon. Lord Devlin

1957 Protection from Power under English Law
    by the Rt Hon. Lord MacDermott

1958 The Sanctity of Contracts in English Law
    by Professor Sir David Hughes Parry

1959 Judge and Jurist in the Reign of Victoria
    by C.H.S. Fifoot, Esq.

1960 The Common Law in India
    by M.C. Setalvad, Esq.

## The Hamlyn Lectures

1961 British Justice: The Scottish Contribution
by Professor Sir Thomas Smith

1962 Lawyer and Litigant in England
by the Rt Hon. Sir Robert Megarry

1963 Crime and the Criminal Law
by the Baroness Wootton of Abinger

1964 Law and Lawyers in the United States
by Dean Erwin N. Griswold

1965 New Law for a New World?
by the Rt Hon. Lord Tanley

1966 Other People's Law
by the Rt Hon. Lord Kilbrandon

1967 The Contribution of English Law to South African Law:
and the Rule of Law in South Africa
by the Hon. O.D. Schreiner

1968 Justice in the Welfare State
by Professor H. Street

1969 The British Tradition in Canadian Law
by the Hon. Bora Laskin

1970 The English Judge
by Henry Cecil

1971 Punishment, Prison and the Public
by Professor Sir Rupert Cross

1972 Labour and the Law
by Professor Sir Otto Kahn-Freund

1973 Maladministration and its Remedies
by Sir Kenneth Wheare

1974 English Law—the New Dimension
by the Rt Hon. Lord Scarman

1975 The Land and the Development; or, The Turmoil and the Torment
       by Sir Desmond Heap

1976 The National Insurance Commissioners
       by Sir Robert Micklethwait

1977 The European Communities and the Rule of Law
       by Lord Mackenzie Stuart

1978 Liberty, Law and Justice
       by Professor Sir Norman Anderson

1979 Social History and Law Reform
       by Professor Lord McGregor of Durris

1980 Constitutional Fundamentals
       by Professor Sir William Wade

1981 Intolerable Inquisition? Reflections on the Law of Tax
       by Hubert Monroe

1982 The Quest for Security: Employees, Tenants, Wives
       by Professor Tony Honoré

1983 Hamlyn Revisited: The British Legal System Today
       by Lord Hailsham of St Marylebone

1984 The Development of Consumer Law and Policy—Bold Spirits and Timorous Souls
       by Sir Gordon Borrie

1985 Law and Order
       by Professor Ralf Dahrendorf

1986 The Fabric of English Civil Justice
       by Sir Jack Jacob

1987 Pragmatism and Theory in English Law
       by P.S. Atiyah

1988 Justification and Excuse in the Criminal Law
       by J.C. Smith

## The Hamlyn Lectures

1989 Protection of the Public—A New Challenge
by the Rt Hon. Lord Justice Woolf

1990 The United Kingdom and Human Rights
by Dr Claire Palley

1991 Introducing a European Legal Order
by Gordon Slynn

1992 Speech & Respect
by Professor Richard Abel

1993 The Administration of Justice
by Lord Mackay of Clashfern

1994 Blackstone's Tower: The English Law School
by Professor William Twining

1995 From the Test Tube to the Coffin: Choice and Regulation
in Private Life
by the Hon. Mrs Justice Hale

1996 Turning Points of the Common law
by the Rt Hon. The Lord Cooke of Thorndon KBE

1997 Commercial Law in the Next Millennium
by Professor Roy Goode

1998 Freedom Law and Justice
by the Rt Hon. Lord Justice Sedley

1999 The State of Justice
by Michael Zander Q.C.

2000 Does the United Kingdom still have a Constitution?
by Anthony King

2001 Human Rights, Serious Crime and Criminal Procedure
by Andrew Ashworth Q.C.

2004 Legal Conundrums in our Brave New World
by Baroness Kennedy of the Shaws

# THE HAMLYN TRUST

The Hamlyn Trust owes its existence to the will of the late Miss Emma Warburton Hamlyn of Torquay, who died in 1941 at the age of 80. She came of an old and well-known Devon family. Her father, William Bussell Hamlyn, practised in Torquay as a solicitor and J.P. for many years, and it seems likely that Miss Hamlyn founded the trust in his memory. Emma Hamlyn was a woman of strong character, intelligent and cultured, well-versed in literature, music and art, and a lover of her country. She travelled extensively in Europe and Egypt, and apparently took considerable interest in the law and ethnology of the countries and cultures that she visited. An account of Miss Hamlyn by Dr Chantal Stebbings of the University of Exeter may be found, under the title "The Hamlyn Legacy", in volume 42 of the published lectures.

Miss Hamlyn bequeathed the residue of her estate on trust in terms which it seems were her own. The wording was thought to be vague, and the will was taken to the Chancery Division of the High Court, which in November 1948 approved a Scheme for the administration of the trust. Paragraph 3 of the Scheme, which closely follows Miss Hamlyn's own wording, is as follows:

> "The object of the charity is the furtherance by lectures or otherwise among the Common People of the United Kingdom of Great Britain and Northern Ireland of the knowledge of the Comparative Jurisprudence and Ethnology of the Chief European countries including the United Kingdom, and the circumstances of the growth of such jurisprudence to the Intent that the Common People of the United Kingdom may realise the privileges which in law and custom they enjoy in comparison with other European Peoples and realising and appreciating such privileges may recognise the responsibilities and obligations attaching to them."

The Trustees are to include the Vice-Chancellor of the University of Exeter, representatives of the Universities of London, Leeds, Glasgow, Belfast and Wales and persons co-opted. At present there are eight Trustees:

From the outset it was decided that the objects of the Trust could best be achieved by means of an annual course of public lectures of outstanding interest and quality by eminent Lecturers, and by their subsequent publication and distribution to a wider audience. The first of the Lectures were delivered by the Rt Hon. Lord Justice Denning (as he then was) in 1949. Since then there has been an unbroken series of annual Lectures. A complete list of the Lectures may be found on pages ix to xii. The Trustees have also, from time to time, provided financial support for a variety of projects which, in various ways, have disseminated knowledge or have promoted a wider public understanding of the law.

The 54th series of lectures was delivered by Baroness Kennedy of the Shaws at the Institute of Advanced Legal Studies of the University of London in November and December 2002. The Board of Trustees would like to record its appreciation to Baroness Kennedy and also to the Institute which generously hosted these lectures.

**March 2003**                                 **BARRY A.K. RIDER**
                                               *Chairman of the Trustees*

# TABLE OF CASES

A, X & Y v Secretary of State for the Home Department [2002]
    EWCA 1502; [2003] 2 W.L.R. 564, CA ........................ 8

Curlender v Bio-Science Laboratories 106 Cal App 3d 811 ......... 34

Detroit Free Press v John Ashcroft 2002 FED App.0291 p.06 ........ 9
Douglas v Hello Magazine Ltd (No.1) [2001] Q.B. 967; [2001] 2
    W.L.R. 992, CA ......................................... 24

Liversidge v Anderson [1942] A.C. 206, HL ...................... 4

McKay v Essex AHA [1982] Q.B. 1166; [1982] 2 W.L.R. 890, CA .... 34
Miranda v State of Arizona 1g 66. 384 US 436, 86 Supreme Court
    1602 ................................................... 18

R. v Department of Health Ex p. Source Informatics Ltd [2001]
    Q.B. 424; [2000] 2 W.L.R. 940, CA ........................ 24
R. v Kelly, February 20, 2001 ................................. 26
R. (on the application of Abbasi) v Secretary of State for Foreign
    and Commonwealth Affairs [2002] EWCA Civ 1598; [2003]
    U.K.H.R.R. 76, CA ...................................... 17

Terminiello v City of Chicago (1949) 337 US 1 ................... 3

W v Egdell [1990] Ch. 359; [1990] 1 All E.R. 835, CA .......... 23, 26

X v Y [1988] 2 All E.R. 648; [1988] R.P.C. 379 ................. 23

# 1. Taking Liberties—Terrorism and the Rule of Law

## A. INTRODUCTION

Thomas Paine: "He that would make his own liberty secure must guard even his enemy from repression."

In the wake of September 11, 2001, still reeling from the horrifying events, I received a telephone call from an American friend—a passionately liberal New Yorker—whose first words to me were "to hell with civil liberties." It was a carefully designed curse because we both knew that surrender of such a household god could not come easily. However, in the face of such a devastating assault upon ordinary, decent people in her city on such an incredible scale, she wanted no truck with the cool reason of law and rights. She was still listening to the long moan of pain emerging from those whose husbands, sisters, sons and lovers were killed. She wanted every young Arab on the turnpike rounded up and she boldly declared she was not averse to a bit of cruel and inhumane treatment if it drew intelligence of future attacks.

In debates about civil liberties, the emotional power is always with those who are suffering. Advocacy for the victims of crimes is easy. And it is invariably at its most potent when our audience can readily imagine themselves being the victim. Few people are concerned to imagine what it might be like to be a young law-abiding person of Arab background falsely arrested; easier to imagine the smoke filling our lungs, the heat of the flames on our skin, the crushing fall of masonry, the leap from skyscraper heights into oblivion.

The problem for civil libertarians is that authoritarians always have the best rhetoric. They claim the songs, the flags, the pictures of the dead and the dying. They claim the role of protector and patriot. They promise a comforting paternalism to which we can surrender and they persuade us that the sacrifice of liberty is worth the warm blanket of security. They will not allow *us* to become victims. With the taste of fear in our mouths, who are we to mount a challenge. As Bob Dylan sang: "Freedom's just another word for nothing left to lose.'

Arguing the cause of civil liberties needs more time than the allotted sound bite. The short attention span of the news roundup impoverishes civic debate. A discourse on rights sounds cold, abstract and legalistic and, of course, that is precisely law's purpose to introduce reason and rationality into the passionate stuff of human existence. But it can leave the arguments bereft of the empathy factor, that is unless you are a young suspected Arab, or Muslim or his mother. The prosecution case is invariably the one that captures the headlines—woman raped in her own bed, child abducted, old lady robbed, wedding party bombed.

One of the reasons why it is hard to engage popular support for the protection of civil liberties is that we are losing our historic memory about the need for such safeguards. Most middle class white people in the West have not for a generation had anything directly affect their lives, which creates the visceral feel for what those protections mean. Of course, there are exceptions. For Jews and the Irish, for black people, homosexuals and other minorities there may still be some sense of what it is like to be powerless and marginalised, at risk of being caught up in a backlash where the law may be your only shield. But in our current climate even minorities who have in the past been at the receiving end of state abuse have been drawn into the warm embrace of "us" as distinct from "them" in the current climate. Even the sixties and seventies generation which so vociferously campaigned for civil rights and liberties is often itself the author of many incursions, no longer able to identify with the targeted groups perhaps because they seem particularly alien.

We in Britain have had our own traumatic experiences of terrorism and made many mistakes in our attempts to deal with it. We should have learned lessons in the process but for some reason we keep revisiting the same follies, forgetting that we have always gained greatest ground when we have adhered to the rule of law.

The rule of law has marked each faltering step towards civilising of the human condition. A structure of law, with proper methods and independent judges, before whom even a government must be answerable, is the only restraint upon the tendency of power to debase its holders.

History is dogged by the tragic fact that whenever individuals, political parties or countries become powerful there is a temptation to refuse to subordinate that power to wider and higher law. As Thomas Aldrich put it "the possession of unlimited power will make a despot of almost any man. There is a possible Nero in the gentlest creature that walks."

The phenomenon of terrorism is one of the great challenges to the rule of law. The temptation for those in government to jettison or erode the rule of law in the face of such provocation is great. Yet it is crucial to recognise that terrorists seek to stimulate precisely such repression. If great care is not taken, emergency measures to combat terrorism end up undermining the very freedoms a country values. Ill-considered laws can be seriously counter-productive in that they help to keep alive and in some cases exacerbate the antagonisms which underpin the political violence. Subjecting terrorists to draconian special laws and to repressive procedures also makes it easier for those who have bombed and maimed to claim to be political prisoners rather than criminals.

Special counter-terrorist laws also set up a contagion which seeps into the interstices of the legal and political system, playing havoc with the mindset of officers and legal function-aries. As a result we begin to lose sight of liberty's meaning in other areas of criminal justice, quite unconnected with terrorism. It is no accident that so many miscarriages of justice took place back in the 70s and early 80s, particularly in the West Midlands and Metropolitan Police and they were not all related to subversion. A culture was created which fostered a particular kind of policing and a neglectful, cynical political class.

This is not to say that a democratic society cannot respond to political violence by the enactment of special laws or the modification of certain evidential rules; it would be perverse if a democratic nation had to prove its liberal bona fides by allowing itself to be destroyed by its enemies. Justice Jackson of the US Supreme Court[1] made the same point "we cannot allow our constitution and our shared sense of decency to become a suicide pact." However, any changes or responses to terrorism which are introduced must conform to the rule of law and the principles which underpin that concept.

The important thing for all of us to remember is that the rule of law is not simply what a government says it is: obeying rules that you have formulated yourself is no great discipline. Even in recent months the Italian parliament has passed laws which will have the practical effect of preventing the prime minister Berlusconi from being prosecuted for criminal charges. It is a form of state capture. There is profound concern that the rule of law is being held up to ridicule, with a premier and his party making laws for their own protection. The rule of law is not the same as rule by law.

Law's purpose is to provide us with sets of rules which should apply when powerful emotions are unleashed. As A.C. Grayling the philosopher points out in his book The Reason of Things.[2] "one of the chief benefits of due process is that it safeguards individuals against arbitrary arrest and interference by government or their servants. It thus interposes an impartial considered process between citizens and the sources of power in society."

The whole function of law is to provide an effective regime for the resolution of conflict even in the heat of passions. "Amidst the clash of arms the law is not silent".[3]

However, in periods of perceived emergency it is all too easy for the Executive to use it control over a legislative chamber—particularly when a nation is in the grip of horror and panic—to introduce repressive laws. It is very easy for the executive to translate its will into law with little challenge, using the liberal use of whips and guillotined motions to curtail debate. Additionally, a climate can be created where any dissent is deemed unsupportive, soft on terrorism or even unpatriotic. The rule of law is a nonsense if all it means is that officials of the state are required to follow the letter of the law, they themselves having decided what the law is. Systems of law are many and various but it must be possible to identify a set of principles, shared by all developed democratic nations, which are non-negotiable; principles which would define the investigation of terrorism and the detention and trial of terror suspects, even after an event as horrifying as the destruction of the twin towers in Manhattan or the bombing in Bali and the consequent loss of thousands of lives.

It is therefore essential to revisit the rule of law and determine what it does mean in the twenty-first century. In our contemporary world, the rule of law must surely mean more than the demand that laws be clear and precise and that procedures are available to check the power of the state.

# B.   HISTORY OF THE RULE OF LAW

The concept of the rule of law has an evaluative as well as a purely descriptive dimension. It started its life here in England with Lord Coke insisting that even the King, the sovereign lord, is subject to law. Not surprisingly, other countries which adopted common law systems, usually as a result of colonialism, absorbed this notion. However, its central thesis that those who govern should not be outside law's disciplines and there should be restraint upon the arbitrary use of power was very compelling, even beyond common law shores, and by the twentieth century had become adopted as a central pillar of all democracies.

Democratic societies display their commitment to the rule of law in a number of different ways. In the area of crime this is done by having clearly defined laws, circumscribed police powers, access to lawyers, an open trial process, rules of evidence, right of appeal and an onerous burden of proof shouldered by the state. In international dialogue, adherence to such due process is urged upon every nascent democracy. As I travel the world in my role as Chair of The British Council I am conscious of the way in which Britain and the United States are looked to as models states where the rule of law is paramount. That is why it matters so much when we are cavalier with the principles of justice and due process because every embryonic democracy sees parallels which would justify their abandonment of process too.

What has to be recognised is that although countries assert their commitment to the principle of fairness, in different countries it has different meaning. There is no single judicial space. Some countries think nothing of holding people for years before trial. Others provide such low levels of legal aid that practical justice is denied. Some systems have jury trials; others do not. But the important fact is that America and Britain have been held up as the paradigm.

I am seeking to posit a number of propositions.

1. The Rule of Law has to mean more than the traditional procedural concept. In the contemporary world it must also mean respect for human rights and civil liberties.

2. The steps taken by Britain in derogating from Art.5 was unnecessary and a cynical act of coalition with the United States.

3. The detention of suspects here in the UK is contrary to the Rule of Law and the quasi-judicial procedures connected to it create an unacceptable co-option of the judiciary by the Executive.

4. The claim that SIAC is purely an administrative process and therefore need not adhere to criminal justice due process standards is a bureaucrat's conception of human

rights. The idea that an alien is a lesser human being because he is not a citizen is an affront to human rights values and puts a hierarchy on the value of life, precisely what human rights law seeks to end.

5. The detention of men in Guantanamo Bay is a total affront to the Rule of Law.

6. The erosion of human rights and civil liberties in the face of terrorism will corrode our legal system as a whole. We have already seen this with the erosion of the right to silence and the right to jury trial.

7. The retreat from the Rule of Law by Britain and the United States will have a retrograde effect on the democratisation of the developing world. What we do in the developed world matters.

# C. PRELIMINARY ISSUES—TERRORISM OR SELF-DETERMINATION?

In any real debate about the response to terrorism there is invariably the "wicked issue" of when the use of violence might be permissible and morally legitimate. It is an issue which cannot be ducked. Certain types of resistance may be morally right and to label all political violence as terrorism is unhelpful. However, it is impossible to reconcile the different perspectives on who is or is not a freedom-fighter and whether any particular political violence is legitimate. Scholarship on the nature of the "just war", which has its roots in the theology of Thomas Aquinas and St Augustine, makes a distinction between *ius ad bellum*—the right to wage war—with *ius in bello*—the rights and duties of those engaged in war whether it's a just war or not. We do not have to be talking about formal wars to recognise that the way in which a military campaign or armed struggle is conducted is a separate moral question. Many may have sympathy with a cause but abhor, for example, the use of suicide bombing on a civilian population. Whatever arguments groups may have about the legitimacy of their grievances they are usually at their most exposed on the issue of ius in bello. As lawyers we do not have to make a judgement one way or the other on the morality of the goals of different political organisations or their historical or cultural claims to legitimacy. But we ought to be able to secure consensus on the fact that too often struggles are conducted on the battlefield of innocent victims.

The moral principles of *ius in bello* do not apply to violent subversive groups alone. The state too is duty bound to behave in morally consistent ways, whether or not the decision to defend itself is morally defensible. Recent international politics is littered with examples of states that have engaged in terrorist campaigns to preserve their own power. Huge attention is given to subversive terrorism, yet the vast majority of innocent victims of indiscriminate political violence world-wide in the past 40 years have been killed by state forces. Other states confronted with terror all too often respond by becoming terrorists themselves.

If we apply *ius in bello* to the liberal democratic state, the moral dimension is even greater than elsewhere. Governments that claim a clear moral distinction between their authority and that of the subversive groups that oppose them are of necessity to be judged by higher standards than their opponents. An important and substantial difference between the state and the subversive in a liberal democracy lies in the existence in the former of an independent rule of law, to which the authorities are always subject. This is the rule of law, not rule by the executive or the police or the military or the exigencies of the moment. It stands for the fundamental principle that every state actor must conform to certain basic requirements of acceptable behaviour set down not by the actor himself but by some body independent of him or her.

The question then naturally arises as to what are the various aspects of the rule of law by which the forces of law and order are to be bound. The answer really lies in the law of human rights. This was emphasised recently by Lord Woolf in his stunning lecture to the Royal Academy.[4] In most liberal democratic nations, the written constitution of the country concerned sets out the basic principles by which all state agencies are explicitly declared to be bound. Most such documents include a code of basic human rights from which the authorities are permitted to depart in only the narrowest of circumstances. In these countries, therefore, the idea of the rule of law is inseparable both from the written constitution and from the courts where it is further defined. Here in the UK, where there is no written constitution, we look to the common law and now the Human Rights Act. International conventions and protocols also serve as a touchstone.

# D. THE NON-NEGOTIABLES

What are the principles which are inviolable even in the face of terrorist atrocities, when people feel a burning sense of

7

outrage. It is very easy for any rational consideration to be overwhelmed by an all too human desire for revenge.

Preventing terrorism would seem to be a clear moral imperative and arguments about civil liberties and human rights are vulnerable to dismissive accusations of unreality and vagueness when compared with the tangible effects of violence on the lives of real people. In 1995, Professor Conor Gearty and his colleague Richard Kimbell of King's College, London reviewed emergency legislation, which had been introduced in the UK to deal with the "Irish Troubles". They evolved the three principles of equality, fairness and human dignity as the objective and immutable yardsticks against which the legitimacy of any such legislation must be judged. Together they represent the basic common denominator of a civilised rule of law and in my view they encapsulate the idea of justice. Even in the environment of international, border-crossing terrorism, for me they remain the best set of principles.[5]

Yet within a couple of years of our creating our own Human Rights Act, inaugurating a new culture of rights we are prepared to trim the whole concept.

The clearest illustration of this is the power to detain foreign nationals indefinitely without charge or trial which the government pushed through a hesitant parliament last December.[6] This is plainly incompatible with human rights obligations, particularly Art.5 of the European Convention and Art.9 of the International Covenant on Civil and Political Rights.[7] The Government claimed a derogation or exemption from Art.5. Derogation is permitted only in time of war or other public emergency threatening the life of the nation and even then only to a minimum extent and consistently with other international obligations. The Special Administration Appeals Commission led by Mr Justice Collins held the attempted derogation failed because it was not only discriminatory—therefore failing the test of equality before the law—but also disproportionate. He did not uphold the argument that there was in fact no state of emergency.

However, his brave decision was overturned by the Court of Appeal[8] and the case is now journeying to the House of Lords.

In times of high political fever it is the judiciary and lawyers who have the control function. The judges have to curb governmental excess; they are the guardians of the rule of law, and it is crucial that they do not allow themselves to be co-opted by the Executive. Detention without trial can become punishment and only judges should be able to punish.

Sometimes, judges can be unwittingly collusive in the erosion of the rule of law by allowing themselves to be appointed to quasi-judicial bodies which adjudicate *in camera* on issues which should be in the public domain. They themselves often become unable to give due regard to the principles which should be the muscle within the rule of law because, unconsciously, they identify too readily with the state or the government of the day. The balancing of human rights considerations against those of state security becomes impossible, often because they too do not have access to all the possible information, but also because they feel they have to give the state the benefit of the doubt. In doing so they can provide a veneer of legitimacy to processes which fall short of international standards of human rights.

Fortunately some judges resist.

An article in the New York Times on September 2, 2002 started:

> You want an American hero? A real hero? I nominate Judge Damon Keith of the United States Court of Appeals Sixth Circuit. Judge Keith wrote an opinion handed down last Monday by a three-judge panel in Cincinnati, that clarified and reaffirmed some crucially important democratic principles that have been in danger of being discarded since the terrorist attacks last September 11. The opinion was a reflection of true patriotism, a twenty-first-century echo of a pair of comments by John Adam nearly two centuries ago. 'Liberty,' said Adam, 'cannot be preserved without a general knowledge among the people.' And in a letter to Thomas Jefferson in 1861, Adam said 'Power must never be trusted without a check'. Last Monday's opinion declared that it was unlawful for the Bush administration to conduct deportation hearings in secret whenever the government asserted that the people involved might be linked to terrorism. The Justice Department has conducted hundreds of such hearings, out of the sight of the press and the public. In some instances the fact that the hearings were being held was kept secret. The administration argued that opening up the hearings would compromise its fight against terrorism. Judge Keith and the two concurring judges in the unanimous ruling took the position that excessive secrecy compromised the very principles of free and open government that the fight against terror meant to protect. 'Democracies die behind closed doors,' wrote Judge Keith.

The court accepted that there may be points within hearings when the administration could argue for the court to go into camera but that should be decided on a case by case basis.[9]

That case shifted the climate of silence in the United States where people felt afraid to speak out about what was happening to their legal system; there is now much more open debate.

Judge Keith was lauded as a hero; we have our equivalent heroes, reminding government why the judicial control function is necessary to curb abuse of power and to protect the rights of those who might be unpopular and marginalised. Doing so may make the judiciary unpopular at times but that is their crucial function in a democracy.

Another fundamental denial of rights inherent in the new anti-terror laws is the prevention of proper representation by lawyers. There cannot be real legal representation if lawyers are not given access to the evidence against their clients. Back in 1984 Michael Mansfield and I represented a member of MI6 called Michael Bettany on charges of attempting to give secret information to the Soviets. There was material which the security services did not want defence lawyers to see—we were tempted to take it personally but we were assured by the then Attorney-General that he too was being denied access because it was so hyper-sensitive. The particular charges had to be dropped because Mike and I went to the Bar Council and indicated that we felt professionally compromised because our ability to properly defend was being undermined.

So far 11 non-UK nationals have been arrested and detained under Anti-Terrorism Crime and Security Act 2002 (Nationals have been arrested under the Terrorism Act 2000 but most have been released without charge or released on bail). The names of all the non-citizens are covered by a UK contempt of court ban and cannot be published. Two volunteered to be deported. Another has been released. One of the remaining eight, Mahmoud abu Bideh, a Palestinian refugee and torture victim, has been removed from Belmarsh to Broadmoor Psychiatric Hospital as he is suffering from Post Traumatic Stress Disorder and is seriously unwell. Psychiatric authorities at Broadmoor recommended against Rideh's transfer to them because in their considered opinion detention in a high security mental hospital is not conducive to his recovery.

The lawyers in these cases are not having an easy time. It is the duty of lawyers to assert their clients' rights without fear or favour, challenging infringements of rights through the courts. If they are denied the reasons for the Secretary of State's decision and cannot test whether the decision is reasonable, the process cannot be just. A detainee can appeal against the Secretary of State's certificate to SIAC (the Special Immigration Appeals Commission) who can confirm the detention or nullify but detainees and their legal representatives are excluded from the hearing.

Last year Lord Steyn was clear in his view that the suspension of Art.5 "so that people can be locked up without trial when there is no evidence on which they could be prosecuted is not in present circumstances justified."[10] There's a hero.

How can the detention of suspected terrorists under broadly drafted powers, seriously restricted procedural protections and very limited recourse to the courts be regarded as consistent with the rule of law? This is arbitrary preventative detention and the antithesis of legality. The Australian High court declared a similar preventive detention measure invalid because it turned the court into an appendage of the executive.

# E.   A NEW LEGAL REGIME?

Ever since the events of September 11, 2001 in the United States, the question has been posed as to whether a new legal regime needs to be invented to engage with phenomenon of international terrorism. Indeed it was claimed by the American Deputy Assistant Attorney General John Yoo that "What the Administration is trying to do is create a new legal regime". Were the laws of criminal justice inadequate or too restrictive upon states seeking to protect citizens? Were the laws of war inappropriate when the enemy was amorphous and not con- fined to identifiable states? As Professor Ronald Dworkin has conceded the line between a conventional enemy power and an international terrorist group is fuzzy. The constitutional lawyer, Phillip Bobbit, maintains that Al Queda is a *virtual* state[11] which is why it should be treated as such in the war against terrorism.

> The multinational terror network that Osima bin Laden and others have assembled is a malignant and mutated version of the market state. Like other states, this network has a standing army; it has a treasury and consistent source of revenue; it has an intelligence collection and analysis cadre; it even runs a rudimentary welfare programme for its fighters, and their relatives and associates. It has a recognisable hierarchy of officials; it makes alliances with other states; it declares wars.

It sounds to me more like a multinational corporation.

Whether or not Al Queda operates like a virtual state, I remain to be convinced that a new legal regime for international terrorism is required. (It is more likely that we are dealing with a stateless band of a few hundred people but with support from many other Islamic groups). However, I do acknowledge that new procedures are necessary. What is essential is that any state confronted with terrorism must decide what existing legal regime it is applying; the laws of war or what are essentially the laws of the criminal justice system of its own nation. What

11

cannot be acceptable is the creation of *ad hoc* legal regimes, pieced together in the face of events, as we have seen in Guantanamo Bay or the passing of anti-terrorist legislation against no backdrop of principle. Severely criticised after the Bali atrocity for its failure to act against extremists, Indonesia quickly passed new Anti-Terrorist laws—what do we think it will mean in a place like Indonesia, where the rule of law is a very fragile concept.

# F. THE PRINCIPLES OF EQUALITY BEFORE THE LAW, FAIRNESS AND RESPECT FOR HUMAN DIGNITY

Can terrorism be defined? Different legislation in different jurisdictions has attempted the task but finding an acceptable definition of terrorism is very difficult. I do not think we have to go there. I think it is sufficient to recognise that even where there is a legitimate struggle against oppression or movement for self-determination, there are always *means* which are impermissible. Terrorism is not and never has been in itself a criminal offence. However, those who commit terrorist acts are committing acts which fall within the definitions of crime. They commit murder, attempted murder, criminal damage—the list is endless. By that, we mean that they fulfil all the elements of those crimes. But, unless we accept the thesis of Bobbitt, as non-state actors they cannot wage war in the acknowledged legal sense. To develop some hybrid process in which the best of both legal regimes is surrendered is to undermine the values for which civilised nations stand.

Many liberal democracies have faced the dilemma of how to deal effectively with political violence and most have sought to stigmatise the actions by using the criminal label. That was an option open to the United States. If this is the adopted course, what has to be established is the extent to which a state confronted with terrorism can and should depart from normal legal safeguards without jeopardising the essence of the rule of law.

In dealing with terrorism the police and intelligence services need to be empowered. Few would resist the creation of tougher laws coupled with heightened security and surveillance. Controlling the revenue stream is far more important than capturing any one individual—but it is corporate money men who do not want offshore safe havens examined because so much tax avoidance will be revealed. New technologies, sophisticated methods of money laundering and ease of travel make terrorism hard to combat. Citizens in developed liberal democracies, who have enjoyed growing freedom, are having to consider what incursions into their civil liberties they will countenance. Counter-terrorist campaigns inevitably involve some invasion of privacy and surrender of rights formerly enjoyed: searches on entering public buildings, the ever-present eyes of CCTV, proofs of identity, forfeiture of sharp objects before air travel, monitoring of internet sites. In investigating terrorism we would expect greater vigilance at ports of entry, the expansion of police powers to investigate bank accounts and e-mails, the changing of thresholds for obtaining search warrants, expanded intelligence gathering, electronic evesdropping and surveillance. This trade-off by citizens of personal freedom for greater security is understandable. However, no change should be countenanced which involves, detaining people without charge and the right to judicial review, or the lowering of standards when seeking to establish guilt.

The principles of equality before the law and fairness require that we extend the same rights to everyone brought into our systems of criminal justice. Whenever we deny to one class of suspects rights that we treat as essential for others, we act unfairly, particularly when that class is politically vulnerable, or identifiable racially or by religious or ethnic distinction. In a state of emergency the principle of equality before the law should require, at the very least, a very clear case that there is no alternative but the reliance on special powers or procedures.

There are important questions for the legal community to ask about what departures from legal norms are acceptable. Would a state be justified in lowering the burden of proof so that conviction might be based on the balance of probabilities? (Professor Lawrence Tribe has argued that while it may be right in more normal times to allow 100 guilty defendants to go free rather than convict one innocent one, the arithmetic should be reconsidered when one of the guilty might blow up the whole of Manhattan.[12]) Would it be acceptable to erode the right to silence by drawing inferences of guilt from a failure to answer questions either during interrogation or at trial (the right to silence was emasculated first in Northern Ireland in 1988[13] and this erosion of the right was extended into the general criminal domestic law of the UK in the Criminal Justice and Public Order Act 1994)? Is it ever acceptable to deny access to the lawyer of one's choice? We must ask ourselves whether is it fair to subject suspected terrorists to a higher risk of unjust conviction? Would a state be justified in lowering evidential standards by admitting hearsay, ignoring the need for corroboration, accepting confessions obtained in oppressive circumstances?

The answer to all those questions must surely be no.

Yet there are problems for the state where they have intelligence reports, which cannot be revealed because the life of their informant may be endangered but which indicate that the detainee is an active terrorist, or conspirator.

The accused may be the best person to challenge the validity of information, having knowledge that exposes the weakness of intelligence reports. The sources of information are all too often people with a grievance or people who perceive a benefit from helping the security services, perhaps because they themselves are refugees. Intelligence may also be coming from countries with highly questionable policing and intelligence-gathering methods. The quality of such information should be a cause for hesitation because the risk that such testimony is false is very high.

However, should the state protect its own intelligence sources by refusing to make such evidence available to the accused, yet allowing it to go before the court *in camera*? Does such a step undermine the concept of fairness and, if so, is such unfairness justifiable in the interests of safety and security?

The argument made by governments is that a trade-off is necessary between civil liberties and security. However, the language of trade-off or balance is misleading as most citizens will not be required to make the trade. It is the rights of the "other", the alien that are being traded.

In all the deliberations of legal change or modification, it should be acknowledged that short-term security victories purchased at the cost of long term political estrangement are not successes at all. There are rarely law and order solutions to essentially political problems. It is also important to recognise that steps taken to counter terrorism have the horrible tendency to creep insidiously into the general fabric of a nation's law, creating new paradigms of state power. As I have said, we have seen this happen as a result of our own experience in dealing with Northern Ireland. There is no doubt that the current drift in the UK away from civil liberties has its roots in that conflict and the lowering of thresholds to deal with the threat. So the notion that such changes relate to "others" should not provide too much comfort.

So how do we proceed if we are not going to roll over in the face of terrorism?

Any legal modifications should be tested against the concept of proportionality. Are the new laws reflective of pressing social need? Are the reasons for it necessary and sufficient? Could alternative methods be used which are less abusive of civil liberties and involve fewer departures from the ordinary legal arrangements. Is the deleterious effect of the law in terms of human rights and civil liberties proportionate to its value to the security forces? In Britain we have a whole raft of legislation to deal with terrorism. Only last year we introduced legislation which made it an offence do incite, plan or support terrorism elsewhere.[14]

Extended detention may well be permissible in dealing with alleged terrorists but safeguards must exist to ensure that such detention is consistent with human rights and habeas corpus must be available after a stated number of days. Legislation, which departs from the normal rules of law, must be highly specific and targeted.

However, targeting the wrong people is worse than futile. It does nothing to protect the public, damages innocent people and destroys confidence in the government in the end. Civil liberties are not just our protections against injustice but our protections against the anger of those who suffer injustice. It was always said that internment in Northern Ireland was the best recruiting sergeant the IRA ever had.

But what do we do about suspect foreign nationals whom we cannot deport back to their country of origin because they would be executed and such an act by Britain would contravene our commitment to human rights? If they are here, and we have sensitive intelligence that they are members of Al Queda, how do we proceed? It may be that the evidence falls short of anything that would stand up in a court of law. It may be that we have good intelligence but we cannot place it in the public domain or let it be seen by the suspect or his lawyer—who is obliged under professional rules to let his client see evidence—because it would be too sensitive. It may be that the intelligence comes from telephone taps or mobile phone satellite interception. Currently, evidence from telephone taps cannot be placed before a court but even the Director of Public Prosecutions, Sir David Calvert Smith, has called for a change in the law to make them admissible. However, if the evidence is not good enough for a successful prosecution or is too sensitive for disclosure there should be no detention.

In Sweden the authorities were presented with precisely this dilemma—do we detain without a proper trial or do we maintain our high evidential standards and the probity of our legal system. They decided that their legal system was too precious for them to depart from principle. They arrested suspects, sought to question them, when met with silence, released them but have kept them under constant surveillance ever since. The suspects know they are being watched and having their calls intercepted 24 hours a day. The Swedes see this as legally preferable and probably no more expensive than the route chosen by Britain.

The Council of Europe's Commissioner of Human Rights has published a report which criticises the UK derogation, pointing out that no other European country sought to introduce such changes in law and it advocates precisely the course taken by Sweden.[15] It is also right that we should be looking at ways of improving extradition pbocedures. However, that does not mean an abrogation of standards. When there is talk of creating better synergies and common modalities it almost invariably means a levelling down rather than up. A legal dumbing-down, if you like. The case of Lofti Raissi showed that very powerfully. Here was a young man arrested on September 21, 2001 in the aftermath of the September 11th events. The US authorities sought his extradition on the basis of suspicions that he may have been involved in the attacks upon the US. It was initially claimed that he was a flight instructor of some of the September 11th hijackers and a co-conspirator in the Al Queda network. On the April 24, 2002 the case against Raissi was halted with the magistrate saying: "I would like to make it clear I have received no evidence whatsoever to support the contention that you are involved in terrorism." He had spent seven months in custody.

# G.   RESPECT FOR HUMAN DIGNITY

The principle of human dignity is directly protective of the basic rights of the individual. What is involved in respecting human dignity is to be found in various international human rights charters including the Universal Declaration of Human Rights. Given the status of such international agreements it is entirely appropriate that anti-terrorist laws should be subjected to scrutiny by reference to them. Respect for human dignity is a common thread running through them all. Of particular relevance is the prohibition on the use of torture or inhuman or degrading treatment. This is why even a true confession should not be admissible in a court of law if it has been procured by torture or oppression. One of the concerns about detaining people in Guantanamo Bay was that it was an intelligence-gathering project, falling outside the normal legal protections. Even the renowned civil liberties lawyer and Harvard Professor,

Alan Dershowitz, seemed to lose his moral compass after September 11. In his new book *Why Terrorism Works*[16] he posited the hypothesis of an arrested person suspected of having knowledge of the existence and location of a ticking bomb. In such circumstances he suggested it should be possible for a judge's order to sanction a little bit of torture. That sort of thinking was precisely what brought the UK before the European Court of Human Rights in the eigthties for its treatment of detainees in Northern Ireland. When asked recently by a young Israeli lawyer what I would do if I was there and then presented with someone I believed had planted a bomb in the building, I told him I would quite probably beat the hell out of him to force him to tell me where it was but I would have to bear the consequences of my actions, particularly if he was some poor soul who knew nothing.

The detainees at the US military's Camp X-ray in Guantanamo Bay, Cuba, include seven UK citizens. The families of two of the men sought to challenge, through the courts, the British government's failure to intervene to protect the human rights of their sons. The court had to decide to what extent an English court can examine whether a foreign state is in breach of its treaty obligations or public international law where fundamental human rights are engaged. They also had to decide to what extent the decisions of the executive in the field of foreign affairs are justiciable and in what circumstances the courts could properly seek to influence the conduct of the executive where it may impact on foreign relations. The legal team argued that the continued detention of their clients at the camp without charge or trial and without access to lawyers is an affront to the values which underpin Anglo-American jurisprudence.[17] While the court turned the application for relief down, they did accept in argument that Abassi and the others were in a legal black hole and that this amounted to arbitrary detention. Although they did not accept there was a duty on the Foreign Secretary to exercise diplomacy on behalf of the men they did assert that "Where fundamental human rights are in play, the courts of this country will not abstain from reviewing the legitimacy of the actions of a foreign state."

Legally, Guantanamo is being treated as a no man's land.[18] It is not in US territory, even though it is leased from Cuba by the American government, and the American government argues that neither the Constitution nor any other US law applies there. The Cuban courts have no jurisdiction. The Americans also argue that the Geneva Convention does not apply because this is not conventional war and the detainees are not entitled to the status and protections afforded prisoners of war. America's own 5th amendment rights guarantee the right to silence and the right to the presence of an attorney[19] but quite intentionally that right does not run in Camp X-ray.

# H.  CONCLUSION

Adherence to the rule of law and human rights does not prevent the passing of counter-terrorist legislation. However, the principles of fairness, equality before the law and human dignity are the touchstones against which such legislation should be judged. Finding and punishing those who commit terrorist outrages is vital. September 11 and the Bali bombing were crimes against humanity—Prosecution of those who commit crimes against humanity is entirely appropriate for state authorities seeking to enforce the criminal law, even where the crimes have taken place outside their territory. That is why it is so important for countries to give their domestic courts jurisdiction over crimes against humanity as we in the UK have now done. It is also the reason why it is so essential that we establish a International Criminal Court and it is disappointing to see Britain roll over, joining with other European nations to exempt the United States from the obligations of engagement.

The nature of a government's response to terrorism within its borders will depend on the type of violence, its history and roots, its seriousness, the extent to which it has community support, and the effect on the international community's respect for human rights. Sensitive political judgements have to be taken. The way in which mature legal systems deal with subversion or attack has global implications: infringements of civil liberties give poor signals to those nations which are struggling to establish democracies. They also give succour to tyrants who have little interest in the rule of law or the pursuit of justice.

We have increasingly a global economy and a global society. By comparison, the global polity is seriously underdeveloped. A workable democratic structure of international law will be more a guarantor of peace and security than displays of power and might.

Law is one of the keys to salvation!

The animating vision of Western democracies in their foreign relations should be of a world of law and consent. That vision has to be rooted in principles of civil liberties and human rights because it is in the noble territory of civil liberties and human rights that the law becomes poetry.

[1] *Terminiello v City of Chicago* (1949) 337 US 1.

[2] A.C.Grayling, *The Reason of Things* (Weidenfeld and Nicholson 2001).

[3] Lord Atkin, *Liversidge v Anderson & anor* [1942] A.C. 206.

[4] Lord Woolf, *Human Rights: Have the Public Benefited?* The British Academy 2002.

[5] *Terrorism and the Rule of Law.* A Report on the laws relating to political violence in Great Britain and Northern Ireland by Professor C.Gearty and J.A.Kimbell. CLRU, King's College London.

[6] Anti-Terrorism Crime and Security Act 2001.

[7] Human Rights Act 1998 incorporating the European Convention on Human Rights into English law.

[8] *A, X & Y & others v Secretary of State for the Home Department* 2002 EWCA 1502.

[9] *Detroit Free Press et al. v John Ashcroft et al.* 2002 FED App. 0291 p.06.

[10] *Human Rights: The Legacy of Mrs Roosevelt*, The Holdsworth Club of the University of Birmingham 2001.

[11] Phillip Bobbit, *The Shield of Achilles.* (Knopf 2002).

[12] Professor Ronald Dworkin, *New York Review of Books*, 2002.

[13] Criminal Evidence (NI) Order 1988.

[14] Terrorism Act 2001.

[15] Opinion 1/2002 of the Commissioner for Human Rights, Mr Alvaro Gilrobles. Strasbourg August 28, 2002 CommDH 2002.

[16] Alan Dershowitz, *Why Terrorism Works*, Yale p.271.

[17] *Feroz Abassi and anor v The Secretary of State for Foreign Affairs* 2002.

[18] In July 2002 3 detainees in Cuba applied for judicial review of their status before a US Federal Court—2 UK nationals and 1 Australian—the judge ruled that the US had no jurisdiction.

[19] *Miranda v the State of Arizona* 1g 66. 384 US 436, 86 Supreme Court 1602.

# 2. Pandora's Box—Genetics and the Law

Just as the twentieth century was dominated by extraordinary developments in the physical sciences—flight, wireless, television, the computer, the microchip, the splitting of the atom—the twenty-first century will be the era of the life sciences. The revolution in genetic science will undoubtedly have a huge impact on our lives. With a greater understanding of disease and disabilities, we can anticipate the development of therapies which will alleviate suffering, provide dramatic cures for illnesses and, through the field of pharmacogenetics, the tailoring of medical and drug regimes to suit our own genetic profiles. Already the knowledge has radically affected the investigation of crime and is beginning to have implications in the field of reproductive choice.

It is inevitable that new knowledge about the human condition will have reverberations in our relationships, not just with each other but also in our connections with the state. Law's purpose is to regulate human relations. Therefore, wherever there are major advances in fields of human endeavour, the law is likely to have a role.

## A. PRIVACY

The genome offers a high degree of information about a human being. With the exception of identical twins, the DNA of each human being is unique. However, we must be careful not to confuse the perceived value of genetic information with its actual value. Genetics is not the scientific version of Mystic Meg where the date when you will turn up your toes is written in the ether. There are relatively few monogenetic diseases: Huntingdon's disease and phenylketonuria are the paradigm cases and even these can be difficult to predict with certainty. Most disease is multifactorial—affected by the environment, lifestyle and other considerations, including the complex interaction with other genes. The time of onset even in single cell disorders is very difficult to predict with any certainty. Negative tests must also be interpreted with caution, as a person who tests negative may still go on to develop the disease. In fact, genetic information rarely provides certain and precise information about a person's medical future. Geneticists are not going to put women with large hoop earrings and crystal balls out of a job for a while yet.

So why all the fanfare? First, despite the present reservations on predictability, we may be able to interpret genetic information with much greater accuracy in the future and what our genome certainly provides currently is some information in the form of probabilities about personal health and traits.

Secondly, genetic information does have special value for a person and his or her relatives, because it is so relevant to medical and reproductive decisions. It is also a very powerful indicator of paternity. Outside of the family, medical researchers hope to use genetic information to find correlations between genes and public health, which can be the basis for therapeutic advancement. Currently, a national research project by the MRC and the Wellcome Trust, called Biobank, is being created which intends to collect some 500,000 anonymised genetic samples from members of the public for epidemiological studies.

But there are other parties who have their eyes to possible uses of genetic profiles. Insurers and employers think the information is useful when it clearly predicts future illness or disability. Schools may also be interested, where genetic information indicates the presence of behavioural traits such as attention-deficit disorders and IQ. Prospective adoptive parents may want the child they are considering adopting tested. The police and other intelligence gathering authorities see potential not only in using DNA for identification purposes but for profiling those with traits for violence.

Although people and organisations are gradually learning more about the limited reliability of genetic information not everyone can be trusted to interpret and use it accurately or fairly.[1] There are legitimate concerns that insurers and employers might presume in error that genetic information is an solid indicator of illness and increase premiums or refuse employment. Medical professionals may pass on information to the health department, which may in turn share it with other government departments. These other departments might use the information in criminal investigations, child support cases or immigration decisions.

Understandably most individuals have a strong interest in the confidentiality, quality and security of their information. Many people also believe that an individual has an intrinsic interest in the control of information about themselves. A question for lawyers is whether the law is equipped to deal with the public's concerns in the context of genetic technology. Does the law protect genetic privacy?

A few years ago President Clinton visited Birmingham for a G7 Summit. He took a photo opportunity, drinking some real ale in a local pub. After the President left, one of his security men paid for the beer, adding the price of the glass from which the President had been drinking, and then carefully slid the item into a holdall before his own departure. Ever the criminal lawyer, this snatch of information in a newspaper induced some interesting speculation on my part. The Monica allegations were still raw, and murky accounts of semen stains on a blue dress had surfaced. Perhaps the President's cohort was protecting his interests. DNA on the rim of a glass had figured in one of my own cases. Alternatively, perhaps the security agent's secretion of the glass was for a sinister purpose, unknown to the President. Hillary Clinton has always maintained that her husband was the victim of a concerted right-wing attack, with powerful forces at work to ruin him. Rather like the Queen warning Paul Burrell of dark forces. I suspect the word REPUBLICAN is the bogey both feared. If I had the time and the talent maybe the beginnings of a novel lurked in there somewhere, but in the meantime I simply harboured the incident as an indicator of the fear even a President entertains that his DNA in the wrong hands could be used unfairly against him.

Imagine if the security agent had not collected the glass but the publican sent the President's saliva off for analysis and sold the genetic information to a tabloid newspaper or to those with access to the famous blue dress? Would the law in England provide the President with a remedy?

In England there are currently two relevant sources of civil liability and some minor criminal offences. The Human Genetics Commission has recommended that the government considers introducing a criminal offence with stronger penalties to deter deceitful and surreptitious collection of genetic information. This would supplement current laws, providing further deterrence and symbolic condemnation of genetic trophy hunting. It would also better protect young children from inappropriate paternity testing, which can occur without adults' consent or court ordered procedures (Liz Hurley and Mr Bing).

The relevant civil laws are the equitable action for breach of confidence[2] and the Data Protection Act. At a quasi-constitutional level, Art.8 of the Human Rights Act applies[3] (the right to respect for family life and privacy, home and correspondence). Traditionally equity protected only confidential information that was imparted within certain relationships of trust, like the doctor-patient relationship. However, a series of recent cases confirmed that the law protects confidentiality in circumstances where there is no special prior relationship but where an obligation of conscience arises from the way in which the information was communicated or obtained[4] (Catherine Zeta Jones and Michael Douglas' marriage deal with OK magazine). The general test is whether a reasonable man in the shoes of the recipient (*i.e.* the publican and subsequently the newspaper) would have realised that the information was confidential. Exceptions apply when the subject consents or disclosure is in the public interest. In our Clinton example it is likely that the publican and the newspaper would be liable in equity, depending on the court's assessment of the public interest value. When it comes to determinations of what is meant by the public interest, the devil is in the detail of each case.[5] What sort of genetic information would the public be entitled to know about? Could it be argued that the health of world leaders ought to be in the public domain if they have their finger on the nuclear button? Or if a political leader advocates strong family values would it be acceptable to expose the fact that they have had extra-marital sex or have fathered children whom they have not acknowledged? In the absence of the public interest exception, equitable remedies would apply if a breach of trust was found to have taken place.

The Data Protection Act provides a more accessible avenue of civil liability but again it is comparatively toothless when the stakes are high. It provides that a person must not process health information unless the data subject has given explicit consent. The publican in the Clinton case breaches this provision when he sends the beer glass for analysis, as does the tabloid on publication, unless, having regard to the special importance attached to freedom of expression, they establish that publication would be in the public interest.[6] An affected person can seek compensation from a court or request that the Information Commissioner carry out an investigation.[7] The Commissioner can then issue an enforcement notice, if the Act has been contravened, and if there is non-compliance there can be a fine of up to £5,000. Normally compensation is only payable for economic damage, but it will also be available for distress in cases where the contravention was caused in journalism. However, the Commissioner's powers are unlikely to deter a tabloid newspaper which thinks it has the goods on a miscreant President. If the Human Genetics Commission's recommendation for the creation of a new criminal offence was accepted it would not only seek to deter the more notorious cases involving public figures but also the more likely situation of an estranged husband having a child tested on an access visit without any consents, or a mother-in-law, who suspects the truth of her grandchild's paternity surreptitiously sending hair samples for testing. The devastation wreaked on children and other family members by revelations made without proper preparation, support and counselling can be long-lasting. Yet this is the area to date where I have received most poison pen letters, all from men who think the feminist lobby is depriving them of their rights, when in fact the concern of the commission was with the rights of the child.

# B. CONSENT

It is important that the wider implications of genetic testing is understood before people consent to a test. Genetic testing can reveal unexpected information and clinicians should recognise that people have an entitlement *not* to know as well as a right to know. The requirements of medical confidentiality need to be clearly understood at all levels and across the entire medical and biomedical research field. Adherence to confidentiality should become an essential part of employment contracts and of membership or relevant professional bodies. This will probably have to be backed by sanctions and possibly the creation of a broader offence against breach of medical confidence.

It is going to be impossible to create special protocols for the handling of genetic information by medical practitioners because it is part and parcel of the whole patient profile and soon, with the wide use of information storage technologies, test results will be interwoven into the fabric of our medical records. The potentially sensitive nature of this information underlines the importance of protecting the confidentiality of patient medical information in general.

A serious concern is that if solid walls do not remain around this medical information people will not have themselves tested through the orthodox channels of GPs and hospitals but will use the internet and over the counter services which they assume will provide anonymity. This will not be in the interests of overall healthcare of the individual patient.

One of the central themes in this set of lectures is my concern about the erosion of public trust, when civil liberties are encroached upon, and the cost of such erosion to society. Inside Information, the Human Genetics Commission's report on privacy, sets out a concept of genetic solidarity and altruism. Sharing our genetic information can in some circumstances give rise to opportunities to help other people and for other people to help us. It is about reciprocity. We have a common interest in the benefits that medically based genetic research can bring.

Rather like blood donation, the gift has a return benefit. However, people want to have confidence that their liberties will be protected if they contribute to the common good and participate in the creation of a medical databank. Society should in turn provide some guarantees. Not only should there be independent oversight of such databanks but it should be illegal to use genetic research databases for any purposes other than medical research. This restriction is important in view of the case law on medical confidentiality. In *W v Edgell* the inmate of a secure hospital was applying for release and his solicitors sought a psychiatric report from the good Dr Edgell to support the application. The doctor was so convinced that the applicant was as mad as a hatter and likely to burn down Liverpool if given his liberty, he promptly released his report on W to the tribunal without the consent of the patient. The High Court decided that the public interest outweighed Mr W's privacy. In another case, *R v Kelly*.[8] The Scottish High Court held that the Scottish Crown could compel pathologists to testify about an inmate's HIV status, despite the fact that the information was collected for a public health purpose and the inmate was given an assurance of confidentiality. The blood samples taken for HIV testing were reversibly anonymised and the Crown was able to de-encrypt the results (the Cambridge Professor Ross Anderson is very clear that there is no such thing as unbreachable information security systems. Anything can be de-encrypted).

In *Kelly* the judge rejected the arguments of unfairness holding that the "public interest is quite clear . . . serious crime should be effectively investigated and prosecuted." Neither case went up the Court of Appeal so the moment, it is, therefore, uncertain whether medical researchers could confidently guarantee that it no circumstances whatsoever would they disclose the identity of Biobank participants. Criminal investigation warrants could override them and, given the current trend to privilege "law and order" issues over civil liberties, it is not impossible to imagine attempts to breach the walls of anonymity.

The Government's approach to liberty has been exposed already in the field of genetics with the introduction of new legislation, The Criminal Justice and Police Act 2001, without adequate parliamentary discussion or public debate. It will allow the authorities to take DNA from virtually everyone who is arrested. This is done by simply swabbing the inside of the cheek with a cotton pad. The DNA will remain in the database forever, even if the person is acquitted of any crime. If your brother is on the database, in many respects you too are on the database as you probably share a huge percentage of his DNA. Anyone who volunteers a sample in an intelligence trawl for the purposes of elimination—for example everyone in a block of flats—will be asked to sign a consent form and their DNA will also remain in the possession of the state. This includes the husband of a rape victim, who gives his sample to assist in isolating the attacker's DNA. The Attorney General agreed that even a victim's DNA would remain on the database if they consented at the time of the investigation. Not surprisingly there are serious concerns as to whether any such agreement given in the heat of an investigation could constitute informed consent. Members of the public know that to refuse to consent to a voluntary sample will draw down suspicions of involvement. Yet no mechanism will exist to apply for removal of your sample after a period of time.

Underlying the process seems to be the cynical belief that those who are connected in anyway whatsoever with a crime are likely to be involved in further offending. In addition, the new provisions exponentially increase the bank considerably. The aim is to hold the profile of nearly one in every 15 people in Britain. Already lawyers involved with the black community fear that ethnic minorities are going to feel disproportionately affected by this method of enlarging the database. Huge numbers of people picked up by the police in their youth but acquitted of any crime will remain on the database for life.

This takes Britain to the top of the illiberal league table: nowhere else in the free world is this happening. Canada and France have already legislated to prevent the retention of samples from persons acquitted of crime and in both jurisdictions samples of juvenile offenders will be destroyed once young people reach adulthood if they remain crime-free for a set period of time. The FBI in the United States has expressed jealous amazement that this legislation was coming into force in Britain, clear that the American public would find such inroads into civil liberties wholly unacceptable despite the heat of their feelings about crime control. Sir Alec Jeffreys, the British professor who invented DNA fingerprinting in 1985 has been very forthright in his criticism of the changes in a recent article in

New Scientist magazine. In his view it is so illiberal and unjust to create a bank by stealth, it would be fairer to take the DNA profiles of every Briton rather than mingle the fingerprints of the guilty with those of the innocent. Other geneticists are also aghast, amazed that the public has seemed to be so supine in the face of such invasion of privacy.

Professor Robert Williamson and his colleague Rony Duncan, geneticists at the Murdoch Children's Research Institute in Melbourne, Australia, also advocate retained tests of "everyone or only the convicted" in the interests of fairness.[9] In reality the public have had little opportunity to absorb the implications of this policy change, as there has been hardly a murmur of public debate. As I said in the lecture last week, the impoverishment of public discourse, the political spin, the media's time imperatives mean an illusion of open democracy is created. Barely any discussion took place about DNA retention in the Commons and despite our best efforts in the Lords, the clauses rattled through.

In a recent case, the Court of Appeal had to balance individual privacy and the benefits of retaining unconvicted persons' DNA samples in the fight against crime. According to Lord Woolf LCJ in his recent Royal Academy lecture[10] particular attention was paid to the evidence on behalf of the police, because the court felt the police were in a better position than it to assess the scale of the contribution which the samples could make to the prevention of crime.

There is no doubt that advances in genetic science are providing a very powerful and effective tool in the investigation of crime. DNA testing is the most important advance in forensic science in our generation and probably in the whole of history. It has considerable public support for such purposes. DNA samples found at the scene of the offence can be highly probative evidence in determining the identity of an offender. The DNA at the scene can take many forms. It may be semen on the clothing of a victim, a speck of blood on a door handle, saliva on a cigarette, a hair follicle, flakes of dry skin or skin cells from a fingerprint. A bar-code is created from this DNA sample, which can be compared with the bar-code created from the DNA sample of a suspect, or a trawl of the database can take place and comparisons may throw up a match. The bar-code is made from non-coding sequences so in itself it gives no information about the phenotype or appearance of the individual. Sometimes it is referred to as junk DNA.

Occasionally the methodology used for comparison is questionable or the technician making the comparison can be mistaken, but in most cases a positive comparison is fairly conclusive evidence. Though it should be recognised that the presence of some DNA at a scene may not prove an accused guilty. For example, in most rape cases accused men do not deny their presence or the fact of intercourse, so DNA is rarely controversial in rape cases because the issue is almost invariably one of consent.

The DNA bar-codes are kept on a computer and the DNA samples from which they are culled are kept in a data bank. The Home Office claims that the retained samples allow the authorities to conduct further tests should the computer fail or if the bar-code is faulty. It also could be subject to further tests for research or other purposes. There is no doubt that as the science develops the police would like to test samples at the scene to produce a profile of the suspect—a tall, red-haired male, carrier of Tay Sachs disease, therefore probably Jewish (Tay Sachs is a comparatively rare disease most prevalent amongst Ashkenasi jews), who may have a history of mental illness, because he is a carrier of a behavioural gene for schizophrenia. The implications for the sense of security of citizens and the potential for authoritarian, invasive conduct by arms of the state is enormous.

Already in New Zealand in a murder investigation, the courts have allowed police access to all the hospital-stored Guthrie tests, which are tiny blood pricks taken from the heel of newborn babies for medical reasons. The access enabled the identification of the killer and I suspect it has not yet been done here only because the police have not thought of it.

The question which immediately follows is "Why not?" to which the answer is "after proper debate and safeguards, maybe yes." Perhaps we should consider a national data base. But only if the public consent. If people give consent for one purpose it should not be abused. Professor Peter Taylor Gooby of Kent University (Social Policy) points out though that DNA matching is probabalistic rather than positive. The larger the numbers on a database the greater the risk of a misleading match.

So questions are increasingly arising. Can we trust the security of databanks and databases in our high-tech world? Who can access our genetic information, and who are the gatekeepers? Already it is being suggested that that there are genes for different aberrant behaviour, such as aggression. There can be little doubt that investigators of crime would see the potential of a data bank. If a DNA sample at the scene of a crime shows the offender carries the gene for a rare disease, could there be a trawl of the medical records, or the Biobank, or the police DNA samples bank, for those with genetic diseases? Recent health legislation allows the Secretary of State to give permission for accessing medical records if it is in the public interest as he sees it (s.60 of the Health and Social Care Act 2001). This means that the procedures are already in place to allow police investigating crime to apply to a politician, so that computerised medical records can be trawled. Given the courts' precedents that the investigation of crime trumps privacy, it looks as though use of medical and research databanks may not be off-limits, unless the government recognises the impact of such incursions on levels of public trust.

Of course Ministers dismiss any Big Brother ambitions. They also insist that the innocent having nothing to fear. Why should we be alarmed that police or other investigators might have sight of our private records if we are decent law abiding folk?

Not surprisingly one of the fears is that once there is access, even for authorised police purposes, there is the risk of the leeching of information to other interested parties for uses that we ourselves do not as yet understand (now I may be sounding a bit like the Queen with her "powerful forces beyond our ken"!).

As the welfare state is being rolled back most of us will be required to make greater provision for ourselves in old age through insurance. For this reason the insurance industry is very keen to know whether we are at risk of living long but very dependent lives. The interest is less on when we might die but whether we might live to our dotage in need of expensive support and care.[11] So people should be aware of potential uses of DNA not yet publicly discussed.

Another recognised fear is related to wrongful convictions— of which we have our own all too recent experiences. People are frightened of being wrongly convicted as a result of cross-contamination, or even an error in the testing process, and they are petrified of being set up for a crime they did not convict. Unfortunately as this science becomes demystified, the possibilities of planting evidence and other abuses will become all too apparent to rogue policemen and other agents of the state.

It is not surprising that it is eminent geneticists like Jeffreys and Williamson who express concern about the potential abuses of a forensic databank full of our samples. They know that genetic tests have become extremely sensitive in the last 10 years. Gene amplification techniques now allow a unique DNA fingerprint from just a single nucleated blood cell. While they argue that in the interests of equity a bar-code of all citizens should be made at birth, what they also insist upon are very real safeguards. The key safeguards are that once the bar-code is made from non-coding sequences, the sample is immediately destroyed. So there would be no forensic databank of samples at all. Secondly, the database of DNA data must be held independently of police.

Here in the UK, the National DNA Database is kept by the Forensic Science Services, the old Home Office labs now liberated from such direct connection. The government expresses complete confidence in the Forensic Science Services, which no doubt do their best to act wholly responsibly. However, no one knows what the future holds. The Human Genetics Commission ("HGC") has recommended that in order to increase and maintain public confidence there should be an independent body, which would include lay members to oversee the way the National DNA Database works.

It is crucial that a climate of suspicion does not develop which creates reservations amongst citizens about voluntarily submitting to DNA intelligence screens when a serious crime has taken place. If fears are not allayed, the public is also less likely to participate in important medical research projects like Biobank. For this reason the HGC is recommending that the Home Secretary makes a statement in the House indicating clearly that the police and intelligence services will make no crime investigation use of Biobank in any circumstances.

Interestingly, in debate the Attorney General asserted that he would willingly give a sample to assist the police if a child in his village was the victim of a crime—as would most decent citizens if they were sure that there was no cost to their doing so. However, the Attorney resisted my enquiry as to whether all Cabinet Ministers would start the ball rolling by putting their DNA on the database. It is worth noting that the police themselves have shown marked reluctance to be included for elimination purposes in case the information might be used in paternity suits, or by the Child Support Agency or in disciplinary proceedings.

The Home Office has agreed to review the processes for the holding and storage of genetic material for criminal investigations.

Concern about the erosion of civil liberties is dismissed as the pre-occupation of liberal intellectuals who are cushioned from the worst vagaries of crime. I have a sad memory of Dukakis standing as Democratic candidate for the American presidency and being vilified as a card-carrying member of the Civil Liberties Union. Yet the same sort of sneering language is now used here in Britain by former champions of our liberties.

There is little discussion about the rationale for civil liberties as a protection for citizens against abuses of power. These safeguards are the mortar which binds a citizen in his or her relationship with the state. When each civil liberty is thrown over, we subtly alter that relationship. The corrosion of trust, which is likely to follow, will ultimately mean a huge cost to good governance. Civil liberties are not just there to protect individuals or minorities who could be subject to harassment, they are there to maintain social cohesion. They are a common good.

However, as I have pointed out, individuals increasingly fear encroachment by other wielders of power. As the state seeks to shrink, power slides into invisible spaces. It is not only government and representatives of the state who might make use of our genetic information in ways which could be adverse and unfair.

The HGC found little evidence of genetic discrimination by employers at the present time. The problem may be more widespread in the United States where medical insurance and employment are so linked. In a case that was litigated recently, employees of a US railway company alleged that the company had discriminated against them by sending blood without their consent to be tested for a genetic marker indicating predisposition to carpel tunnel syndrome (a disease that affects the wrists and the arms). The medical examination applied to 36 employees who had filed claims or internal reports of work related carpel tunnel syndrome injuries against the company. The company had hoped to defend the action on the bases that the workers were genetically predisposed to the syndrome so they should not be held liable. The employees sued the pathology lab as well as the railway company, under the Americans with Disablities Act 1990. Once the underhand testing was discovered the company reached a confidential settlement with the plaintiffs.

Genetic discrimination in the context of insurance has been a more potent public controversy in the UK. This has been the subject of several independent inquiries in the past decade and early this year the HGC recommended a temporary moratorium during which time insurers will rarely use genetic tests to assess premiums. An exception applies where the applicant applies for life insurance valued at more than £500,000 or critical illness insurance valued at more than £300,000 and the genetic test which the insurer uses has been approved by the Genetics and Insurance Committee.[12] The moratorium is proposed as a temporary measure until further policy analysis is completed. Further questions include:

- Would a prohibition cause standard premium prices to rise dramatically thereby forcing economically under-privileged people out of the insurance market?

- Should the prohibition apply to family history information or diagnostic tests, which indirectly reveal genetic information?

- Should an inhibition apply to general medical histories which also result in differential premium pricing?

- Are the caps set on the value of assurance that falls under the prohibition set at a fair level?

- Is specific legislation required or can policy be managed through "smart" regulation on a co-operative basis by government and the Association of British Insurers.

These issues are unlikely to come before the courts unless legislative reform is passed. Insurance contracts must be *"uberimmae fides"*—in the utmost good faith—with full disclosure from the proposer. Accordingly the insurance applicant must disclose genetic tests which they know may be materially relevant to premium pricing.[13] The insurer has the discretion whether to dismiss the requirement to disclose potentially relevant information. The disability Discrimination Act 1995 has little impact. It defines discrimination narrowly and provides that a person is considered to have a disability only when their impairment has a substantial adverse affect on day-to-day activities. Therefore the Act fails to protect persons who are discriminated against because of a pre-symptomatic genetic trait. The situation is different in Australia, where in most states legislation prohibits discrimination based on a disability that exists, or may exist in the future.[14]

It is difficult to conceive of a common law action which would protect individuals in the absence of an applicable statutory definition. For this and other reasons the HGC is recommending that the government consider separate UK legislation to prevent genetic discrimination. What is interesting is that the anxieties about insurance, for example, make powerful arguments for why a National Health Service ("NHS") is a blessing—with health care for all unconnected to private insurance. It also may take us down the road of considering social insurance, rather than private insurance, to deal with the long-term care issue. Socialist solutions may yet have their day. You wait.

However, in many other ways current legislation and the common law provide adequate remedies, albeit new challenges for the judiciary.

It is arguable that there is a need for codification of the rights of children and parents after a mix-up by the fertility clinic or negligent provision of services. The common law is quite unclear. There is a marked difference between the approach of courts in Australia and England for example in the relevant area of "wrongful life" claims by parents.

Consider for example the case where a doctor fails to notice that an embryo carries a genetic mutation that predisposes it to serious mental retardation. Instead of implanting another embryo, he inserts the embryo into the mother's womb. Although causation is clear (the harm could have been avoided by choosing another embryo or foregoing pregnancy on this occasion) the liability for damages remains unclear. Presuming the parents are the complainants, current UK precedent suggests that parents should recover only for the extra costs of treating or managing the disability. Other jurisdictions have departed from English precedents. An action for negligent pre-birth genetic testing is more complicated if the action is brought in the child's name. Courts have tended to perceive such cases as actions for wrongful life. That is, they understand the child to be saying "the doctor negligently failed to diagnose my condition. But for his negligence I wouldn't have been born with this disabling condition". But at the same time the child is saying "but for the doctor's negligence, I wouldn't have been born at all. Another embryo would have been gestated in my place". It therefore means that the child is asking to be compensated for being born. Such a case has succeeded in the US.[15] But English courts have held that life, even with severe birth defects is not a compensable injury for a child.[16] Pre-natal screening is already a routine procedure and no doubt will become extensive as pre-natal genetic diagnostics develops. In future there may be greater numbers of complaints about failed diagnosis of genetic disease and consequent law-suits. Under current law the only plausible action lies widh the child's parents. The distinction between actions by a child or a parent is arguably untenable and we may see major upheaval in this area of law. This would mean amending the Congenital Disabilities (Civil Liability) Act 1976. On the other hand, perhaps legislation is unnecessary or undesirable. The law may simply need time to develop. It may be best to allow this to happen incrementally through case law.

However, there are serious financial implications for the medical profession and the NHS as genetic testing develops. The potential for legal actions for failure to detect or advise patients about genetic traits are very real and it is my view that we should be revisiting the idea of a "no fault" compensation system. The pursuit of perfection particularly in reproduction will create unbearable pressures on the medical profession. We can be sure the courts will be asked to compensate for the lack of genetic enhancement patients feel they have been promised: the musical ability, the academic genius, the physical prowess. A newspaper article just this week exposed that young female students were selling their eggs to pay off their student loans and other debts. Given that the current source for many eggs is from women described as elderly *prima gravidas*, there may be a growing market in more youthful supplies.

There is concern that there may be a higher incidence of medical problems for babies conceived from eggs harvested from and then donated by women undergoing IVF treatment—you can just imagine the legal actions for using "past their sell by date" eggs instead of fresh organic eggs from nubile young things.

Let us contemplate one further twist. Recently, a profoundly deaf lesbian and her female partner sought infertility treatment. They requested that they be allowed to use sperm from a family with hereditary deafness, and employ pre-implantation screening to select the embryo carrying the genetic sequence for deafness. That is they requested a deaf child. This has been referred to as designer disability in the press.[17] Or even genetic disenhancement. They argued that deafness is not a serious harm to a child, and moreover it would be in the child's interests to be deaf in *their* family. Putting the ethics to one side, what if their request was allowed but the doctor acted negligently and a child with perfect hearing was born. Would the law compensate them for the fact that the child *has* hearing?

Gene therapy poses other potential sources of litigation. Regrettably a recent incident of harm caused by gene therapy occurred in France. The French team treating children with severe combined immune deficiency has had to call a halt to the gene therapy trial because one of the 10 children has developed what looks like leukaemia. No allegation of negligence has been made but the case shows the risks of gene therapy if it were to be used negligently.

As a result of the experience the French have halted trials but the UK Gene Therapy Advisory committee decided against this course, arguing that parents appraised of the risks should have the liberty to consent to, or withdraw from treatment. Theoretically the judiciary could be asked to rule on whether experimental gene therapy is in a child's best interests. Courts are familiar with the sort of weighting exercise that must be undertaken but such a case would not be easy—it would involve complex and uncertain medical evidence about toxicity and adverse reactions of the gene therapy, as compared with bone marrow transplants. Equally difficult moral judgements are called for regarding the best interests of a sick child. Is the longest life necessarily the best? Perhaps the least painful life is better? Or the most free? Or perhaps the best life is the one where the child and his parents feel in control of their destiny? The judiciary may one day soon wrestle with these questions.

Gene therapy may also pose extremely difficult questions for sports law. You can imagine that one day there may be two classes of competition at the Olympics: one race for the *"au naturel"* athletes and another for the "genetically enhanced." How could sports lawyers identify rule-breakers? Then, of course, there are the issues of saviour siblings—where a child may be conceived using assisted pregnancy techniques and pre-implantation genetic testing, so that the tissues can be a close match to those of an older sibling who is sick. In Britain we have two cases so far. In the Hashmi case the HFE Act gave its permission. There the living child had a rare genetic disorder. Pre-implantation genetic diagnosis ("PGD") for a subsequent baby would have happened in any event. Therefore the tissue-matching was only an additional procedure before choosing an embryo to implant. However, in the case of Whitaker, the living child had a condition which resulted not from an inherited condition, but from a mishap. In such circumstances a parent would not normally be going through the PGD process to select a preferred embryo. In those circumstances the HFE Act withheld consent, conforming to its own protocols that PGD is not a procedure to be used for utilitarian purposes.

There are issues involving "submarine heirs" who surface after a parent has died. It may mean a child making a claim on the estate of its genetic parent. Leaving aside legal technicalities, it may be said that that an innocent child is not responsible for the social arrangements of its birth and should not be deprived of its inheritance. Aside from legal liability, questions of ethics abound in the realm of gene therapy, and often the two are mixed.

In many ways judges cannot avoid being philosophers in this area. Almost all cases involve complex decisions about the interests of children, parents, embryos, possible children, would-be parents, medical professionals, public standards of morality, the common good and the liberties of citizens. Even in cases of basic statutory interpretation, like the case currently going to the House of Lords of therapeutic cloning under the HFE Act, the courts find that they must broach complex public policy issues. That is a case brought by the pro-life lobby claiming that word embryo as used in the HFE Act does not cover embryos produced without sperm. Their purpose is to open up the whole anti-abortion debate again because of their moral objections to these processes. It is therefore important that judges recognise the moral complexion of their decisions, and their public policy implications. They really are jumping into the deep end of the gene pool in some of these areas, and if they do not appreciate the wide consequences of decisions, others certainly will.

Once judges recognise that part of their task is inherently philosophical, in a moral sense, it is another question how they should respond. They will need to think carefully about the nature of morality—for example, is there an objective concept of the good life, or of right conduct? What is the moral status of an embryo? If not, or if we are inherently uncertain about what it would consist of, then judges should be very careful in the way they decide moral and public policy issues. They might impose their own morality on the rest of society. In some cases this could add to the tragedy.

There are different ways judges should proceed. They might seek *amicus curiae* from philosophers of various persuasions, or pressure the democratic arms of government to legislate more explicitly on some of these areas, or require government to create democratically-inspired policy, which might be referred to judges. Alternatively, they might try to discern general principles which, as the philosopher John Rawls said, would be justified as principles, because they would be reasonably agreed by people who recognise the extensive, yet reasonable, pluralism of our society.[18]

The genetics revolution is presenting us with a brave new world. Only today Severino Antinori announced that a cloned baby would be born in the next few months (I still think most people will choose to have babies in the good old fashioned way). Most of the knowledge will greatly improve our lives, whilst some of it brings serious threats, but the wonderful thing about the human condition is that we have always risen to new challenges.

---

[1] Human Genetics Commission, *Inside Information: Balancing interests in the use of personal genetic information*, Department of Health 2002.
[2] X v Y (1988) 2 All ER 648 (QB); W v Edgell (1990) 1 All ER 835, CA.

[3] The right to respect for family and private life, home and correspondence. No public body may act in a way that is incompatible with the Convention rights under the Human Rights Act. Courts can declare Acts of Parliament incompatible with Convention rights.

[4] *Douglas v Hello Magazine Ltd* (2001) QB 967; 1001, CA; *R. v Department of Health Ex p. Source Informatics Ltd* (2001) QB 424, 438, CA.

[5] G. Laurie, *Genetic Privacy*, Cambridge University Press 2002, 279ff.

[6] DPA, s.32.

[7] DPA, s.42.

[8] *R. v Kelly* (February 20, 2001) High Court of Justiciary, Glasgow.

[9] *DNA testing for all*, Nature, Vol. 418, August 8, 2002.

[10] Lord Woolf, "Human Rights: Have the Public Benefited?" The British Academy, October 15, 2002.

[11] Association of British Insurers, Press Release: "Government Endorses 5 year Moratorium on Genetic Testing and Insuarance. Opportunity to Develop a Lasting Consensus" (London October 23, 2001).

[12] See n.11 above.

[13] See T. McGleenan *Insurance and Genetic Information* (Independent Report for the Association of British Insurers, London 2001).

[14] K.Liddell *Just Genetic Discrimination? The ethics of Australian Law Reform Proposals*, (2002).

[15] *Curlender v Bio-Science Laboratories* 106 Cal App 3d 811.

[16] *McKay v Essex AHA* [1982] QB 1166, CA.

[17] Julian Savulescu, *Deaf Lesbians, Designer Disability and the Future of Medicine* (2002) 325 British Medical Journal 771.

[18] John Rawls, *Political Liberalism*, 1996.

# 3. The Benign State—A Modern Myth

Edmund Burke: "The people never give up their liberties but under some delusion."

A few months ago the Home Office Minister for Criminal Justice, Lord Falconer, inveighed against criminal defence lawyers. Apparently, the rise in crime is partly the responsibility of this unscrupulous class of being, who cross examine witnesses at length, spin out trials and assist the criminal classes to avoid justice. The time had come for a victim-led justice system rather than a system weighted in favour of the accused. The attack from Lord Falconer—a commercial lawyer with no real experience of the criminal courts—came immediately after the Prime Minister had called for a re-weighting of the system in favour of the prosecution. According to the Tony Blair "It is perhaps the biggest miscarriage of justice in today's system when the guilty walk away unpunished". In a single sentence the Prime Minister sought to overturn centuries of legal principle, a complete reversal of the approach to justice that every mature democracy in the world respects, whereby the conviction of an innocent man is deemed the greatest miscarriage of justice. For some reason our masters seem set to abandon a number of underlying concepts with an easy stroke, made easier with the carefully orchestrated publication of alarmist statistics suggesting the system is in crisis.

In that same week Paddy Hill, one of the Birmingham Six wrongly convicted of the Birmingham bombing, finally accepted a settlement of his claim against the British government. But he described very poignantly how financial compensation could never repay him for the destruction of his life wrought by a false accusation, wrongful conviction and 17 years in jail.

It is as though the occupants of high office have no memory, no sense of residual shame at the system's failure, a failure which should have convinced us all that protecting those accused of crime from wrongful conviction remains one of the highest priorities of the state and that all too easily those acting on behalf of the state can corrupt the process. It seems particularly extraordinary that Labour, which has always passionately championed civil liberties, is now prepared in government to abandon its stewardship of the principles. Of course, along with Paddy Hill's account are the many other powerful, painful stories told by those who experience crime. The position of victims should not be ignored. I have spent my life in the law arguing as vigorously for the rights of those who suffer because of crime as for the accused. Improving the system, particularly for women and children when they are complainants in cases of rape, sexual assault and abuse has been a central plank of my work. And there are many ways in which this can be done. However, I know when a campaign to improve the position of victims is being hijacked to reduce the rights of defendants. Maintaining that justice for victims can only be purchased at the expense of the accused is as dishonest as the claim that jurors are the source of miscarriages of justice. Claiming that what is needed is a levelling of the playing field between those who are the victims of crime and those who are accused of crime is to delude the public about the role of the state.

Criminal practitioners within the legal system, who prosecute and defend, know why civil liberties matter. The principles seep into the bones with every day in court. As Oliver Wendell Holmes, the American Supreme Court Justice said: "The life of the law has not been logic. It has been experience." We know how devastating wrong-judgements can be. Human experience has taught us that rights are indispensible to democracy. However, making the arguments is not always simple because civil liberties constrain the state from enforcing certain majoritarian preferences. If you live by opinion polls and focus groups, they will all be telling you that there is too much crime, the system is soft on criminals and something ought to be done. There is nothing new in the majority of the public holding those views. But the risks attached to majoritarianism are precisely the reasons why protections and safeguards have to exist. What is new, is for a government to mount such a wholesale assault on the underpinnings of the rule of law in this country.

I want in this lecture to pose two questions: Why is *this* government mounting an attack upon civil liberties? Secondly, why *do* civil liberties matter?

The new legislation will remove trial by jury from fraud trials and other complicated financial cases—this is likely to extend to money laundering and importation of drugs with a complex money trail, drawing in financiers. It will allow for a judge to sit alone in cases where there is evidence of jury interference or where there is fear of a jury being subborned.

The new laws will allow juries to be told of an accused's previous convictions so that they will know the kind of person they are dealing with. This means that the presumption of innocence becomes a formula—a legal fiction rather than a reality.

In the early days of New Labour I had tended to think that, as with the economy, the government was anxious to show that it too could play hardball. Labour governments have always had to prove that they are as financially astute as Conservatives, that they too can run the military and are not afraid of war and when it comes to law and order they really have to show their metal, not so much taking no prisoners as taking lots of prisoners. So when I was feeling very pessimistic, I thought the tough talk on criminal justice was just a display of machismo by the boys with just a touch of magisterial snobbery about criminal lawyers thrown in by the caravan of commercial lawyers who now inhabit the corridors of power.

However, I think something more complex is taking place, with the coalescing of a number of policy shifts.

## A. THE POLITICISATION OF CRIMINAL JUSTICE

All governments can be seduced by power; it has a mesmerising quality. "Power is delightful and absolute power is absolutely delightful" as Lord Lester has been known to say. On top of that no contemporary government identifies itself with a potentially oppressive state. Part of the problem is that our governors see themselves as the good guys. "So what is all this old-hat business about the malign power of the state? People who share our values, should know that we would not use our power to bad ends. Trust us." And knowing them as I do, I think they are good guys but I also know that there must always be in place serious restraints on power.

Once people "are the state" or have their hands on the levers of the state they have amnesia about the meaning of power and its potential to corrupt. They forget the basic lessons that safeguards and legal protections are there for the possible bad times which could confront us, when a government may be less hospitable, or when social pressures make law our only lifeline. They forget that good intentions are not enough, that scepticism about untrammelled power is essential. No state should be assumed benign, even the one you are governing. Governments ignore the fact that once liberties have been lost they are almost impossible to restore.

Politics in Western democracies, they say, has moved on. We are now living in a post-modernist, post-ideological state where the potential for extremes of any kind has moved off the political radar. History has ended, as Fukayama asserted,[1] with victory to the free market and parliamentary democracy. In such a world, politics has converged in the centre ground, with parties only pitching slightly leftwards or rightwards; the Western state in such a configured world, they would have us believe, is benign, vanilla-flavoured, posing no real threat to any citizen that cannot be remedied by making an application to the courts under the Human Rights Act.

In his own writings on politics David Blunkett presses this delusion.[2] The state, he tells us, is not some bogey of which we should be afraid. It is in fact you and me, the community. Civil liberties are as much about the needs of citizens to be protected from crime and to live in security as about civil liberties as traditionally defined.

In this brave new Third Way world, government is seeking to find a Third Way approach to criminal justice. However, there is no Third Way when it comes to liberty.

I am still to be convinced that there is any intellectual coherence in the Third Way. There is nothing new about its central tenets. They have been lived for decades in most Western democracies at the heart of social democratic parties—a mixed economy, a regulated market, pluralism, concern for social justice. Renaming a reality has the smack of the PR consultant about it; you have to give your "brand" a name and in our non-ideological world it must have no whiff of socialism about it.

However, in amongst the hype and glib cosmetics, Tony Blair is on to something. There is a need to reposition left politics in a way that makes more room for civil society and the participation of citizens in the solution of social problems. The dead hand of the state should be lifted from people's lives. Ways should be found to engage people. (For conservatives, this is always about voluntarism and faith-based organisations providing services which have formerly been supplied by the state.) But the absence of coherence means that there is a failure to recognise, for example, that the jury system is the best example you can find of a public/private, partnership. By that, I mean the combined forces of the private citizen and the state.

What Labour brings and has brought to government which is so distinctive is a commitment to end discrimination against women and minorities, whether black or homosexual; a widening of opportunities for those who have been disadvantaged by the system, a serious and imaginative strategy for tackling poverty. It has been brave and reforming on many fronts, particularly with regard to the constitution. The introduction of the Human Rights Act is an extraordinary and powerful development. The government is also trying to modernise institutions, which have become moribund and creaky—and the legal system is one of those.

New Labour's warm embrace of the market and its endeavour to thin out the role of the state in the delivery of public services and welfare, calls upon it to chart new waters. The problem is that when they do that they often slide into right of centre positions rather than progressive ones. The government describes its vision as shift away from the Big State, the nanny state, to the enabling state, putting more choice in the hands of individuals. In the sweep of reform crossing all ministries the challenge, as they see it, is to thin out what is delivered by government; citizens themselves or the private sector can assume many of roles formerly undertaken by the state. The state is to step back. In the view of New Labour the Welfare State had created its own vested interests, which would have to be tackled head on—not just the recipients of benefits but hospital consultants, public service unions, legal aid lawyers, state school teachers. In this "post-state" vision, it is easy to make the mistake that criminal justice is another aspect of state provision, ripe for rebalancing, with the state stepping back. What is so disingenuous about the rhetoric of "rebalancing the system" as between victims and the accused is that it presents the criminal trial as a contest between these two parties and is a denial of the central role of the state. What we are, therefore, beginning to see is a semi-privitisation of the criminal justice process, with the victim, the private individual, being used to disguise the reality of the powerplay.

This may not have been the original design but these are the distortions which take place if reform is embarked upon without consideration of wider consequences. Reform is not possible without a compass. You have to start by taking your bearings and deciding what are the non-negotiables.

In his wonderful poem *Seeing Things*, Seamus Heaney describes the hard process of renovating an old building. It contains lessons for anyone embarking on a modernisation process.

Roof it again. Batten down. Dig in.
Drink out of tin. Know the scullery cold.
A latch a door bar, forged tongs and a grate.

Touch the cross-beam, drive iron in a wall.
Hang a line to verify the plumb,
From lintel coping stone and chimney breast.

Relocate the bedrock in the threshold.
Take squarings from the recessed gable pane.
Make your study the unregarded floor.

Renovating the law can be a hard task but in doing so we too must Study the unregarded floor. We have to relocate the bedrock and decide what is non negotiable.

# B. THE NATURE OF THE CRIMINAL JUSTICE PROCESS

The reason for the criminal justice process is to create distance between the grief, anger and understandably vengeful human emotions felt by a victim. The de-coupling of the victim's intimate engagement from the prosecution allows rationality and rules of law to intervene.

The law regulates our social relations. When an individual suffers a wrong or is harmed in some way, their redress is sought through the courts using the law of torts. The claimant and defendant come before the courts as equals. Here we **can** talk about balance as between the parties. (though it may not feel like that if you, the individual are suing some huge corporation. If a Government was really interested in a degree of "rebalancing" here would be fruitful territory.) In the civil courts, the remedy comes in the form of compensation not loss of liberty.

The role of the criminal courts is different. Certain wrongs offend not just against the individual but against society as a whole, undermining the values and mores, which bind the nation, putting at risk social order and community wellbeing. Citizens sign up to a social contract which means acknowledging that their suffering is not just a private matter but one affecting the community as a whole. Individuals are not entitled to punish or exact revenge. The state, however, is entitled to marshall all its resources to prove the crime in a court of law and is entitled to punish—subcontracting the determination of appropriate punishment to an independent judiciary. Because there is such inequality of arms as between the state and the individual, the scales are balanced in an accused person's favour. The state is like a super-charged juggernaut bearing down on a man with a bike. The protections and safeguards are just the provision of a crash helmet.

In the criminal courts the victim is a witness for the state, a crucial witness, a central witness but a witness nonetheless. So when the government talks about rebalancing of the system, it is really about a rebalancing in favour of the state, giving more power to the state. That is the fraud in the Government's rhetoric, the sleight of hand.

Let me immediately make it clear that witnesses have many reasons to be displeased about their treatment by the state in its role as prosecutor—they are often left in the dark about the process, marginalised and sometimes exposed to inappropriate cross-examination. The quality of policing and prosecuting could be greatly improved. Witnesses have many legitimate grievances but they are grievances to be addressed **to** the state and which the state should meet—but not by mounting assaults upon the balances between the state and the accused in the criminal trial.

Improving the treatment of witnesses is an important area for reform and one where we have already seen considerable change in the last decade. However, there will inevitably be occasions when the victim or their family is disappointed because a prosecution fails. Not surprisingly the focus of their anger is the accused when often the real problem may be the absence of strong enough evidence, faults in the investigation and inadequate prosecution. However, since the mediators for the victims are policemen and prosecutors, it is hardly likely they will tell the victim of their own shortcomings or the ways in which prosecution testimony failed to satisfy the standards of proof. The state's failure is, therefore, often seen as the fault of the accused.

# C. THE IMPACT OF THE *LAWRENCE* CASE

There is no doubt that the government's approach to criminal justice reform has been greatly affected by some prominent cases. The murder of Stephen Lawrence, a young black student, has sent shock waves through the criminal justice system ever since he was stabbed to death by a group of white thugs.

It has become a touchstone for the law's failures, replacing the Irish miscarriages of justice as the gauge of police and legal ineptitude.

The manner of the investigation left the Lawrence family with no trust in the system, even parts of the system which were doing their job properly. The Crown Prosecution Service, examining all the evidence before them at the time decided that there was insufficient evidence initially to secure a conviction against the young men suspected of the offence. They were right. There was only one eye witness, Stephen's friend, who had been deeply traumatised by the incident and whose account was, not surprisingly, shaky on some aspects of what took place.

Had everyone waited, the chances are that further evidence would have come to light. Groups of people who swear allegiance to each other *in extremis* have great difficulty remaining silent in the longer term. People talk, people get religion, people abandon old loyalties, people resent being lumped together with others in whispered accusations of guilt if they themselves did not wield the knife. The chance that something would eventually break was in my view quite high. A continuing rigorous investigation was what was necessary. A family carefully supported and kept abreast of each development by the prosecuting authorities would not have felt so marginalised.

The Lawrence family had no trust in what they were hearing because of the way they had been treated. The system's failure derived from stereotypical assumptions about race and the family's anger and distress was wholly justified, as the Macpherson Inquiry showed. The police had been crudely insensitive in its dealings with Mr and Mrs Lawrence making assumptions that Stephen must have been up to no good, perhaps with drugs, in some way authoring his own fate. Nothing could have been further from the truth. However, taking the private prosecution was a mistake. The private route to criminal justice taken in default is always hamstrung because the rules are set for a contest between the might of the state and the individual. The legal advice given to the Lawrence family was folly. But these judgements are always much easier in retrospect. The judge ended up having to enter verdicts of not guilty because of insufficient and unsatisfactory evidence and the men now walk free but are still suspected of having committed the crime.

Undoing the travesty that took place because of a disastrous investigation is virtually impossible. There is currently no new evidence that could justify bringing the suspects back before the court. The documentary film showing the men larking about, simulating a stabbing and speaking in disgusting racist terms, does not prove that they killed Stephen Lawrence. The recent conviction of two of them for a racist assault upon a black policeman does not prove they were murderers. But the more important question is how could any jury be found that would be impartial after the saturation coverage the case has received? Justice is now impossible. The lessons to be learned are about improving police investigation and eradicating racism from the system. They are about giving proper support to victims and their families, establishing trust and giving clear explanations for decisions. Interestingly, the Dando family had only admiration and gratitude for the way the police supported them. The answer to a failure of justice as experienced by the Lawrence family is not to start dismantling the legal protections and principles which underpin the system.

Yet now we have the Government advocating retrial of an acquitted person in serious cases such as murder where compelling new evidence comes to light. The Double Jeopardy rule says that no acquitted person should be put through a trial process again for the same offence. The rule exists as a protection of our liberty. The state should not be able to retry people until it gets the result it wants and to do so is oppressive. There must be finality. To do away with the rule even in serious cases lets the prosecuting authorities off the hook of conducting proper investigations the first time round. But it also opens the gates to incredible media abuse. Imagine the response of the media where there is an acquittal which upsets a victim or victim's family. On the steps of the court there will be a declaration by every family that they will never rest until there is another trial and the accused is behind bars. The police will be under pressure never to close the books on a case.

The Lawrence experience should be serving as a justification of the double jeopardy rule's existence because it is a case which illustrates police failures to investigate thoroughly at the time and the mistake of a premature decision to prosecute on inadequate evidence.

The Government's suggestion is that the retrial of an acquitted person would only take place after judges in the court of appeal consider the new evidence so compelling that a retrial is justified. They cite cases where DNA is discovered after the event yet produce no evidence of such a thing ever happening nor are they confining their argument to the arrival of DNA a highly probative new science. They have now produced a list of 34 categories of crime where the state right to request retrial will be sought. The government says cases tendered for retrial would be few and far between but they would inevitably attract huge publicity. How could there be a fair retrial? A second jury might assume that, since our cleverest judges thought the new evidence was highly persuasive, their role is simply to endorse a conviction. The risks to justice are enormous. The extraordinary thing is that juries are likely to think that if they acquit, the accused can always be brought back with the consequence that we are likely to see more acquittals.

What we are seeing is a strange post-modernist kind of law reform in response to high profile cases like that of Stephen Lawrence and Damilola Taylor and with insufficient thought given to the reasons for the rules. The French call this kind of policy-making ''Le pragmatisme Anglais'' where we change education systems or privatise rail systems and do the research and thinking afterwards. Our politicians seem to be driven by short-term goals which make them oblivious to long-term consequences. What we should have learned from miscarriages of justice is that when the system fails to deliver justice it is usually not because the legal principles have failed us. It is almost invariably because we have failed to live up to the legal principles. The answers are always to be found in better lawyering, judging and policing.

# D.   HIJACKING OF THE VICTIM

This hijacking of the victim by the state causes me some baleful musing about the law of unintended consequences. The victims' movement came out of the women's movement in the seventies and the progress can be clearly charted. Feminist lawyers, like myself, in the United States, Canada, Australia and here, began to turn the spotlight on the way in which the law failed women and particularly examined the experiences of women in rape trials and criminal cases involving domestic violence. From that we expanded the critique to other victims of crime, particularly children. Victims' Support and a variety of other support agencies came into being, widening the focus to the systemic failures, affecting all witnesses going through the courts, whatever the nature of the offence. The issues, therefore, moved into the mainstream, which is a welcome breakthrough.

The introduction of human rights law has also drawn greater attention to the position of victims. It has presented a powerful tool and language to challenge the state that it has a duty to look after their interests. This presents a conundrum for the state. In seeking to protect victims it has to be creative but it also has to be alert to its even greater duty, namely its duty to those who come before courts accused of crime. The state's duty is greater to defendants because the state has the power to punish them, imprison them, take their liberty.

The reason the government has forgotten its responsibilities in this climate of rights is that it sees votes in crime and in women but not when women are committing it, I should hasten to add. It is now very fashionable to talk about the treatment of women in the system but only if they are **victims**. The numbers of women in prison have tripled in the last ten years. Imagine how many more women will end up in prison when magistrates have their sentencing powers increased to two years.

Statistically, women are much more inclined to plead guilty and come before the courts for less serious offences. They are also most often the primary carers of children. Their children end up in care and the cycle of deprivation which leads to crime is set in motion.

When I have argued for the better treatment of women in the criminal justice system, I have always made it clear that justice for women could not be secured by reducing justice for the accused, some of whom are women anyway.

Government sees the force of being seen to improve the position of women in the criminal justice system particularly the victims of rape and domestic violence. Women are a large part of New Labour's constituency. New Labour also wants to position itself as the new national party, reaching into what would have been Conservative heartlands. To do so, it is very responsive to perceived public opinion on law and order, which it evaluates through polling and focus groups. But, unless a discussion of crime very sensitively addresses what might happen to **your** child or **your** son if arrested, and issues about potential victimisation of minorities, loss of social cohesion and risks of wrongful conviction, the general public can lose sight of what the removal of safeguards will mean. The links are not being made. We all want to see less crime and more guilty people brought to book. However, that is not necessarily the same as getting more convictions. The Chinese have well-tried ways of getting more convictions—so do the Indonesians—but human rights and the rule of law are not a high priority.

# E.   JUDICIAL CO-OPTION

We should always be finding ways to oil the wheels of justice, avoiding delays, reducing waiting times for witnesses, keeping costs down where possible—but the good management of courts should not be surrendered to managerialism and the erosion of keystones of the system.

What the government does is slide between substantive issues and process issues as if there was no distinction between them. The Auld Report which was undertaken at the request of three cabinet ministers, the Lord Chancellor, the Attorney General and the Home Secretary, exhibits this same failure to see that some areas of law reform are constitutional and highly contentious politically and, therefore, different from areas of procedural change. The remit offered to Lord Justice Auld was inappropriate and not something to be undertaken by a practicing judge. This elision of substantive and process change has drawn Robin Auld into a co-option by government which, as a judge of the court of appeal, he should not have entertained. It is perfectly appropriate for a judge to advise on procedural reform and refinements, as Lord Woolf did in his reforms of the civil justice system. It is perfectly proper for judges to chair enquiries. But practising judges should not become one man policy think tanks at the service of government, advising changes which mean the removal of substantive rights. Not because judges are not entitled to their views. As Lord Woolf pointed out in his Royal Academy speech he is as entitled as anyone to freedom of expression. Judges can write learned papers and give speeches to their hearts content but they should be mindful that given their roles in a climate which is ready to spin their opinions for political ends they may make themselves vulnerable to challenge in the courts. We need our judges to remain outside the Whitehall embrace.

And here I sound a warning to the judiciary. Judges should give some reflection to any support they may contemplate for the removal of trial by jury in serious cases because once judges alone are deciding guilt or innocence in these cases the judiciary will become much more suspect in the minds of the public. An acquittal of rich businessmen because of want of evidence will bring allegations of executive justice with white collar criminals thought to be getting a different deal. No one knows the names of the jurors who acquitted the Maxwell brothers but individual identified judges will take the flack for decisions, far more so than happens today.

Judges will come under a scrutiny to which they have until now never been exposed. Like politicians their every breath and choice will begin to matter. A judge trying a case alone will be subject to personal profiling. Already investigative companies operate in this area to fulfil business requirements of due diligence and these firms will readily extend their range of business. Obviously as we have become more alert to the significance legally and politically or real or imagined conflicts of interest in the judiciary, a viable market in profiling has presented itself and as we move more and more to a career service for the judiciary these issues are likely to become more pertinent. Every stock and share owned by a judge or his wife, every case with commercial links in his years of practice, the list will be endless.

The Auld Report, stimulated by a call to think the unthinkable, and then cherry-picked by Government for the least expensive reforms means the government can claim judicial approval for profound encroachments on citizens rights. The proper body for consideration of serious changes always used to be the Law Commission, but it seems to be almost completely sidelined now. Co-option of the judiciary by government can be very subtle but it a risk to be avoided at all costs.

# F. TRIAL BY JURY

The government long ago decided to reduce trial by jury—it is a potential reform which has been sitting around in Home Office for decades. Former Conservative ministers have told me that during the Thatcher years it was regularly pulled out and presented by officials for consideration but rejected as too illiberal. So what we are seeing in these reforms is not some radical set of New Labour proposals but recycled Home Office policy bin-ends.

Labour came into government determined to strip its approach to policy of any ideological baggage and has been applying a "what works" test to many of its public service changes.

Lord Justice Auld's report advocated a wide-scale redesign of the court structure, which meant radically reducing the right to jury trial. The government then cherry-picked his report, jettisoning anything too costly or over-complicated, showed how reasonable and third way they are by limiting the reduction in jury trial to fraud and other complicated crime and cases where there may be jury-nobbling.

By reducing the number of jury trials, in fact quite dramatically, we institute an erosion, not only of justice, but of active citizenship. The social contract is about rights and responsibilities and here we have the finest example of just that. The jury tradition is about a duty of citizenship, which gives people an important role as stakeholders in the criminal justice system. Seeing and participating in the process maintains public trust and confidence in the courts and underlines society's connection with its own laws. It is one of the reasons why our criminal justice system is admired around the world. It is also one of the features of our system of law and governance which produces real civic capital—civic capital is not easily reducible to pounds shillings and pence but it is that unquantifiable but hugely important subsoil from which trust is created and from which thriving societies grow. Lots of things contribute to it and in different societies it varies. Sometimes you only realise its importance when it's gone.

Because juries are representative of society as a whole they create a collective wisdom which cannot be matched by a judge sitting alone.

Norman Finkel in his book *Commonsense Justice*[3] describes it beautifully:

> "Rooted in a legal history . . . the jury, the conscience of the community speaks. In calling the law to follow the path of the community, we are not ubging it to heed majoritarian, transitory, ignorant, or unprincipled sentiment. We are asking it to acknowledge what it may have forgotten or lost sight of: the deeper roots of justice."

Or as Jeffrey Abramson said in *We, The Jury*[4]:

> "The direct and raw character of jury democracy makes it our most honest mirror."

What is so interesting are the contradictions in the government's approach. Here is a government wedded to the focus group yet the finest example of the focus group at work is the jury. But, when it comes to crime, juries, the ordinary punters, are to be distrusted.

The doublespeak on this issue of juries is remarkable. According to ministers it is paternalistic to make a whole range of evidence inadmissible because of fears that a jury may misuse the information in a prejudicial way against an accused. Juries are smart, intelligent people and should be given the full facts; they can decide what weight to attach to different kinds of evidence such as hearsay or previous convictions. Yet when it comes to fraud and complicated matters like money laundering, juries are too stupid. Juries do not have the appropriate skills and professional experience.

In a House of Lords debate about reducing jury trial Lord (Gareth)Williams of Mostyn dismissed concerns about erosion of rights, saying that he too had resisted changes when he was a practitioner, such as giving the prosecution the right of appeal on sentences deemed too short or limiting the right of silence so that juries can now draw an inference of guilt from an accused refusing to answer police questions. In retrospect the changes were sensible he suggested and the sky had not fallen on our heads.

Of course, he is right. Taken one at a time, as in a game of pick-up sticks, the system does not collapse with a single reduction, with each thinning down of civil liberties. But slowly the mortar in our democratic architecture is destroyed in ways which are irreparable.

Before such changes should be countenanced there should be evidence produced to show the change is necessary and likely to achieve the desired outcome—reducing crime and bringing those who commit crime to justice. The burden should be upon the government to prove such radical departure from principle is necessary. Like evidence-based medicine, there should be evidence-based law reform.

We are living through a period of huge global change, experiencing the equivalent of shifting tectonic plates. Globalisation is transforming the social, economic and political landscape. The world map has been ideologically redrawn and we are seeing the convergence of many developments which have profound ramifications—microelectronics, computing, telecommunications, broadcasting, genetics. They are transforming our material world in a myriad of ways and the implications for civil liberties are very real.

Multinational corporations are ever expanding their reach. Globalising processes create patterns and power networks, legitimate and illegitimate, that bypass national boundaries and potentially undermine national autonomy—whether it is e-commerce, Americanisation, Islamic fundamentalism, terrorism, the webbing of the internet, economic federalism—the list goes on. All these mean that the nation state no longer feels secure. Citizens within this disturbingly unsettling world seek areas of certainty closer to home. They are prepared to sacrifice a significant level of freedom and privacy in exchange for greater security. The temptation is for governments to read expressions of public fear and this willingness of citizens to make sacrifices as a blank cheque to rewrite underlying principles of law. What governments so often fail to understand is that the founding precepts of law are cultural and located in deeper soil than they credit. To be effective new laws have to resonate with that historic pulse and the value system of a people.

It is clear that the law cannot remain the same in such a period of flux. It too has to evolve to meet the challenges of new times. But the question we must always pose is what are the underlying principles, the non-negotiables in this period of change.

---

[1] *The End of History*, Francis Fukayama.
[2] David Blunkett.
[3] (Cambridge: Harvard University Press, 1995) 337.
[4] (New York: Basic Books, 1994) 250.

# INDEX

**Access to lawyers**
rule of law, and, 5
**Acquitted defendants**
DNA samples, and, 27
**Al Queda**
legal status, 11
**Appeals**
rule of law, and, 5
**Auld report**
judicial co-option, and, 50–51
trial by jury, and, 51

**Biobank**
genetics, and, 22
**Blood donation**
consent, and, 26
**Burden of proof**
rule of law, and, 5

**CCTV**
counter terrorism, and, 13
**Civil liberties**
genetic information, and, 31–32
terrorism, and, 1–3
**Confessions**
equality before the law, and, 14
**Confidentiality**
genetic information, and, 22–23
**Consent**
genetic testing, and, 25–37
**Corroboration**
equality before the law, and, 14
**Counter-terrorism**
equality before the law, and,
11–16
rule of law, and, 3

**Criminal justice**
effect of *Lawrence*, 45–48
introduction, 39–41
judicial co-option, 49–51
nature of the process, 44–45
politicisation, 41–44
role of the victim, 48–49
trial by jury, 51–54

**Data protection**
genetic information, and, 24
**Democratic society**
political violence, and, 3
rule of law, and, 5
**Detention of foreign nationals**
rule of law, and, 8
**Discrimination**
genetic information, and, 32–33
**DNA**
consent, and, 27–28
privacy, and, 21–22
**Double jeopardy**
criminal justice, and, 47

**Electronic eavesdropping**
counter terrorism, and, 13
**E-mail**
counter terrorism, and, 13
**Emergency**
rule of law, and, 4
**Employers**
genetic information, and, 32
**Equality before the law**
terrorism, and, 12–16
**European Convention on
Human Rights**
Article 5 derogation, 8

**Evidence, rules of**
rule of law, and, 5
**Extradition**
equality before the law, and, 16

**Fairness**
terrorism, and, 12–16
**Forensic Science Services**
DNA database, and, 31
**Fraud trials**
trial by jury, and, 40

**Gene therapy**
litigation, and, 35–36
**Genetics**
consent, 25–37
introduction, 21
privacy, 21–25
**Guantanamo Bay**
respect for human dignity, and,
16–18
rule of law, and, 6
**Guthrie tests**
DNA samples, and, 29

**Hearsay**
equality before the law, and, 14
**Human dignity, respect for**
terrorism, and, 16–18

*In camera* **hearings**
equality before the law, and, 14
**Insurance industry**
DNA samples, and, 30
genetic information, and, 32–33
**Interception of communications**
counter terrorism, and, 13
**Interference with juries**
trial by jury, and, 41
**International Covenant on Civil
and Political Rights**
Article 9, 8
**Internet sites, monitoring of**
counter terrorism, and, 13
*Ius in bello*
self-determination, and, 6–7
**IVF treatment**
litigation, and, 35

**Judicial co-option**
criminal justice, and, 49–51
**Jury interference**
trial by jury, and, 41

**Legal aid**
rule of law, and, 5
**Legal representation**
rule of law, and, 10

**Miscarriages of justice**
criminal justice, and
Irish cases, 39
*Lawrence*, 46–47
rule of law, and, 3
**Money laundering**
equality before the law, and, 13
trial by jury, and, 40

**'No fault' compensation**
genetic testing, and, 34–35

**Paternity testing**
privacy, and, 23
**Personal searches**
equality before the law, and, 13
**Police powers**
rule of law, and, 5
**Political violence**
democratic society, and, 3
equality before the law, and, 12
self-determination, and, 6
**Pressing social need**
equality before the law, and,
14–15
**Privacy**
genetics, and, 21–25
**Proof of identity**
counter terrorism, and, 13
**Proportionality**
equality before the law, and,
14–15

**Rape victims**
criminal justice, and, 49
**Representation**
rule of law, and, 10

**Revenge**
terrorism, and, 8
**Rule of law**
historical background, 4–6
introduction, 2–4

**Search of the person**
counter terrorism, and, 13
**Secrecy**
rule of law, and, 9
**Self-determination**
terrorism, and, 6–7
**Sharp objects**
counter terrorism, and, 13
**Silence, right to**
equality before the law, and, 13
**Special Immigration Appeals
  Commission (SIAC)**
rule of law, and, 10
**'Submarine heirs'**
genetics, and, 36
**Suicide bombing**
self-determination, and, 6

**Tax avoidance**
equality before the law, and,
  12–13

**Terrorism**
conclusion, 18
equality before the law, 12–16
fairness, 12–16
introduction, 1–4
legal regime, 11–12
non-negotiable principles, 7–11
respect for human dignity,
  16–18
rule of law, 4–6
self-determination, and, 6–7
**Therapeutic cloning**
ethics, and, 36–37
**Trial by jury**
criminal justice, and, 51–54

**Victims**
advocacy, and, 1–2
criminal justice, and, 48–49

**Wrongful life claims**
genetic information, and, 34